# TALENT ACQUISITION TOOLBOX: STRATEGIES FOR RECRUITMENT AND SELECTION

*Chikwendu Ukachukwu Obioma*
*HR manager and consultant*

**To my late father**

# Contents

# Introduction to Talent Acquisition

*"Recruitment is about making sure you have the right people, with the right skills, in the right roles, at the right time." - Richard Branson*

In this present dispensation, talent acquisition has become the fulcrum and important component of most, if not all, organizations. It is a key factor in determining how well an organization can achieve its goals and objectives. This position has also made it a crucial one within the field of human resources. And the reason for this is not far-fetched, as it involves the strategic process of finding, attracting, and onboarding the right talent to meet an organization's current and future needs. According to Kelvin Wheeler (2021), effective talent acquisition is essential for businesses, as it ensures they have a high-quality workforce that can drive growth, innovation, and success.

When we talk about talent acquisition, it is pertinent that we understand it from a holistic point of view. The process of talent acquisition encompasses various stages, from understanding the organization's talent requirements to onboarding selected candidates. It includes strategic planning, recruitment, screening, evaluating, and selecting the most suitable candidates for different roles within the organization.

Talent acquisition is more than just filling open positions. It is a strategic process that aligns human capital with organizational objectives. If the organizational goals are to be met, then it requires the right kind of personnel with the requisite skills, knowledge, and technical know-how. The reason why most organizations, businesses, and corporate entities are not operating at the level they should is because of a lack of effective and efficient human capital. For an organization to move from point A to point B, it needs a qualified workforce that can steer its wheel and pilot its growth initiative, which is why talent acquisition is at the forefront of most organizational strategies. Once an organization is able to excel in talent acquisition, it automatically attracts individuals who bring diverse skills, innovative thinking, and a passion for the company's mission. This, in turn, positions the organization ahead of its competitors. In the words of Josh Bersin (2023), talent acquisition is not just about finding candidates; it's about acquiring a competitive advantage through people. If we take a census of all the big global companies such as Google, Apple, Samsung, Louis Vuitton, Microsoft, Saudi Aramco, Meta, Exxon Mobile, Telsa, Shell, Visa, and the list goes on, we will find out that they have one thing in common, which is an effective, efficient, and creative workforce. These companies understand that the modern business landscape is dynamic, and for them to survive and continuously strive in such a challenging business environment, they need to acquire talents with the ability to adapt to change, ensuring that the organization can navigate uncertainties and capitalize on emerging opportunities. This statement has been echoed by Elaine Orler (2022), who highlighted that talent acquisition is essential for building an agile workforce, making it a strategic imperative for any goal-driven organization.

As a HR consultant, I have had the experience of witnessing how thriving companies can become redundant because of mistakes made in their hiring process. Most times, it takes years for these companies to bounce back if they are fortunate enough. These experiences and my passion for an effective and efficient workforce propelled me to write down my ideas on how companies and organizations can effectively go about their hiring and recruitment in such a manner that gives them both a competitive advantage and an appreciable amount of ROI. In this book, you will be exposed to the best strategies, channels, and methods that you can use to attract the best talent, as well as how to onboard and retain them. Not only that, you will also learn about the emerging trends and technologies in talent acquisition.

# Chapter one

## Understanding the Importance of Talent Acquisition

*"Investing in talent acquisition is investing in the future. The right hire can be the catalyst for transformative growth." – Michael Lee, HR consultant*

The truth still remains that talent acquisition is crucial and important for organizational success, especially in today's dynamic business environment where businesses are constantly looking for ways to achieve a competitive advantage. So having a good understanding of the importance of talent acquisition is crucial for building a skilled and productive workforce. Like we have already mentioned earlier, talent acquisition involves identifying, attracting, and hiring the right individuals to fill key roles within an organization. Currently, talent acquisition has gone beyond traditional recruitment and is now more focused on long-term strategic planning, ensuring that the right talent, which in this context involves skilled individuals with fresh ideas, perspectives, and expertise, has the ability to drive innovation within the organization. Having a talented workforce enables businesses to respond quickly and effectively to changing market conditions and demands. In addition to that, effective talent acquisition can lead to improved employee retention, increased productivity, and a more competitive edge in the job market. By recognizing the significance of talent acquisition, businesses can effectively align their human capital with organizational goals and objectives.

Some of the benefits of talent acquisition that have been noticed over the past two decades include:

## Employee Engagement and Retention:

Talent acquisition significantly contributes to employee engagement and retention by aligning organizational goals with individual skills and aspirations. When the hiring process is meticulous, it creates the right balance and fit between candidates and the company culture, which gives the employees a greater sense of belonging and purpose.

According to John Sullivan (2023), who understudied the impact of talent acquisition on employee engagement and retention, "acquiring individuals who align with the organization's values and culture contributes to a positive work environment. This, in turn, fosters employee loyalty and reduces turnover, ensuring continuity in achieving long-term goals." Additionally, strategic talent acquisition facilitates professional development opportunities, fostering a culture of continuous learning that enhances job satisfaction and loyalty. Overall, a well-executed talent acquisition strategy contributes to building a motivated and committed workforce.

## Innovation and Creativity:

Acquiring individuals with diverse perspectives and experiences fosters a culture of creativity. Such a workforce is better equipped to generate innovative solutions and drive the organization's competitiveness in a rapidly evolving business landscape. This is the same argument Lou Adler (2022) made when he said that talent acquisition is the catalyst for innovation.

## Impact on the Bottom Line:

Dr. John Sullivan (2023) emphasized that talent acquisition directly influences the bottom line. Quality hires contribute to increased productivity, customer satisfaction, and revenue growth. A strategic approach to talent acquisition ensures that the investment in human capital translates into tangible business outcomes.

## Ensuring a competitive workforce:

In today's dynamic and competitive business environment, having a talented and skilled workforce is crucial for an organization's success. Talent acquisition helps identify individuals with the right skills, knowledge, and experience required for the job, ensuring that the organization remains competitive.

## Succession planning:

Effective talent acquisition involves not only filling immediate job vacancies but also identifying potential future leaders within the organization. Succession planning ensures that there is a pipeline of talented individuals who can step into key roles as and when required, reducing the risk of leadership gaps and thereby creating a seamless transition into critical positions.

## Enhancing organizational culture:

Talent acquisition plays a vital role in shaping the organizational culture. Hiring individuals who align with the organization's values, mission, and vision can contribute to a positive work environment and help maintain a strong culture that attracts and retains top talent.

## Cost savings:

Effective talent acquisition can lead to cost savings in the long run. By ensuring that the right individuals are selected for a role, organizations can reduce turnover rates and the associated costs of recruitment, onboarding, and training. Moreover, hiring individuals with the right skills and experience can result in increased efficiency and productivity, contributing to overall cost savings.

**Building a diverse and inclusive workforce:**
Talent acquisition can help organizations build a diverse and inclusive workforce by actively seeking out individuals from different backgrounds, cultures, and demographics. Promoting diversity and inclusion not only enhances the organization's reputation but also leads to improved decision-making, increased employee engagement, and a broader range of perspectives within the organization.

**Adapting to changing needs:**
Talent acquisition is essential for organizations to adapt to changing business needs and market conditions. It involves keeping up with industry trends and identifying emerging skills and competencies that are critical for the organization's future success. By proactively seeking individuals with these skills, organizations can stay competitive and agile in a rapidly changing business environment.

## The Role of Talent Acquisition in Organizational Success

The best way to understand how important talent acquisition is to organizational success is to take a closer look at the business landscape. Every company is looking for ways to be ahead of their competition, so anything that gives them a competitive advantage is highly welcomed. Companies are going the extra mile and doing what it takes to attract top talent who can easily fit into the job description and carry out their assigned tasks in the most effective and efficient way with the least amount of training. This single act can save most companies a huge amount of money that would have been put into employee training. This is not to say that companies that invest in employee training are wrong, but the idea here is that strategic talent acquisition can help in cutting costs, and the money can be reinvested into other productive ventures. In my work as a HR consultant, I have come to find out that one of the most important aspects of talent acquisition is ensuring that the right people are in the right positions. By thoroughly understanding the skill set and qualifications required for each role within an organization, recruiters and HR specialists can effectively match candidates with appropriate positions. When employees are properly aligned with their roles, they are more likely to be engaged, productive, and satisfied, which in turn translates to improved organizational performance.

Additionally, I have also noticed something worthwhile: there is this realization that talent acquisition has a significant role to play in an organization's employer brand. Employer brand in this context refers to an organization's reputation as an employer and its ability to attract and retain top talent. In today's digital age, it is common knowledge that potential candidates now research and evaluate companies before deciding to apply. Therefore, organizations need to ensure that their employer brand accurately represents their values, culture, and opportunities for growth. Talent acquisition professionals play a crucial role in building and maintaining a positive employer brand by effectively communicating the organization's values and opportunities to potential candidates.

Furthermore, talent acquisition plays a critical role in improving diversity and inclusion within organizations. A diverse workforce not only promotes innovation and creativity but also allows organizations to better understand and cater to a diverse customer base. By actively sourcing candidates from diverse backgrounds and ensuring equal opportunities for all applicants, talent acquisition professionals, recruiters, and HR managers can contribute to creating a more inclusive work environment. When this is achieved, what happens is that it enhances organizational success by fostering greater collaboration, creativity, and better decision-making processes.

To effectively carry out talent acquisition strategies, organizations must employ several key practices. Firstly, organizations should clearly define their talent acquisition goals and align them with their overall business objectives. This ensures that talent acquisition efforts are focused and directly contribute to the success of the organization. Secondly, organizations need to invest in effective sourcing techniques, such as leveraging social media, building a strong employer brand, and establishing partnerships with educational institutions and professional networks. These practices help to attract a diverse pool of qualified candidates. In addition to that, I would want more organizations and companies to prioritize candidate experience throughout the talent acquisition process. This is needed to make the whole process more appealing and satisfactory to prospective employees. My reason for making this suggestion is quite simple. Candidates who had and enjoyed positive experiences during the application, interview, and subsequent on-boarding stages are more likely to accept the job and become engaged employees. By streamlining processes, providing regular communication, and incorporating technological solutions, organizations can enhance candidate experience and significantly improve their ability to attract top talent.

Moreover, talent acquisition professionals such as recruiters, HR managers, and personnel must make it a habit to continuously evaluate and enhance their recruitment strategies to adapt to changing job market dynamics. Staying updated with the latest recruitment trends and technologies is crucial for success in attracting and retaining top talent. By leveraging artificial intelligence data analytics, recruiters and HR managers can streamline their processes and make informed decisions.

To create a clearer picture of what we are saying and enable you to understand the significance of strategic talent acquisition, I feel it is pertinent to examine some notable examples of big corporations and organizations that have achieved success through their recruitment strategies:

1. Google is arguably one of the most successful companies in the last two decades. Irrespective of its success, Google is renowned for its rigorous hiring process, which focuses not only on technical skills but also on cultural fit and creativity. This approach, for me, has enabled the company to consistently attract the best talent in the industry. By fostering an environment that values innovation, Google maintains a competitive edge and continues to develop ground-breaking products.

2. Procter & Gamble (P&G): P&G has had both longevity and success. One of the reasons for this is their strategic approach to talent acquisition. It is a multinational consumer goods corporation that invests heavily in leadership development programs and talent pipelines, aiming to nurture future leaders from within the organization. This strategic approach ensures a continuous flow of skilled leaders to drive the company's success in the fast-moving consumer goods sector.

3. Amazon: Amazon is one of those companies that has successfully developed a customer-centric approach while combining diverse business models. This means that they have a large pool of talents with a wide range of skills, ranging from data scientists to logistics experts. The company hires individuals who contribute to its rapid scaling and dominance in e-commerce. Amazon's ability to diversify into various industries, such as cloud computing and entertainment, is a testament to its strategic talent acquisitions.

4. Salesforce: Anyone who knows about Salesforce will agree with the fact that it is a company that puts so much emphasis on its core values. It is a value-driven company, and because of that, a strong emphasis is placed on hiring individuals who align with its core values. This strategic approach has resulted in a workforce passionate about the company's success and innovation. By attracting top talent that shares its vision, Salesforce has become a leader in cloud-based customer relationship management (CRM).

5. Netflix: Netflix's unique company culture, which values freedom and responsibility, shapes its strategic talent acquisition. The company hires individuals who thrive in a dynamic and challenging environment. This approach has positioned Netflix as a leader in the streaming industry, continuously producing high-quality content and adapting to ever-changing market dynamics.

These examples demonstrate how strategic talent acquisition can translate into organizational success and a competitive advantage.

## Key Challenges in Talent Acquisition

I believe that one of the most profound challenges in talent acquisition is sourcing the right talent. Organizations need to identify the right channels and platforms to reach out to potential candidates. With the advent of technology and the rise of social media, traditional methods may not be sufficient to attract top talent. For example, if a company is looking to hire software developers, it needs to consider leveraging platforms like LinkedIn or participating in coding forums to engage with qualified individuals. Furthermore, many organizations struggle to tap into passive candidates who are not actively seeking new job opportunities. These individuals may possess the right skills and experience, but they can be challenging to reach without a proactive approach.

Another significant challenge in talent acquisition is attracting and engaging candidates effectively. In a competitive job market, potential candidates often have multiple options available to them. Therefore, organizations need to create a compelling employer brand and an attractive employee value proposition to stand out from the competition. This includes developing a strong company culture, offering competitive compensation packages, and providing opportunities for professional growth and development. For example, companies like Google and Facebook have successfully built their brands as desirable employers, attracting top talent from various industries.

Once candidates are attracted, the next challenge organizations face is assessing their suitability for the organization. Traditional hiring methods, such as resumes and interviews, may not always provide an accurate representation of candidates' skills and potential. To address this challenge, organizations need to adopt innovative assessment techniques such as skills-based tests, job simulations, and behavioural assessments. For instance, companies like IBM and Unilever have integrated gamified assessments into their talent acquisition processes to evaluate candidates' abilities and cultural fit accurately.

Moreover, retaining top talent after recruitment is a persistent challenge for organizations. Invested time and resources in talent acquisition can go to waste if employees leave shortly after being hired. To combat this challenge, organizations need to focus on creating a positive employee experience and implementing effective retention strategies. This includes providing a supportive work environment, offering career progression opportunities, recognizing and rewarding performance, and fostering a healthy work-life balance. Examples of successful retention strategies can be seen in companies like Airbnb, which offers unique employee perks and benefits, and Salesforce, which prioritizes employee well-being and engagement.

Lastly, the rapidly evolving business landscape has led to a growing need for specialized skills and knowledge. This creates a challenge for organizations to identify and acquire talent with the required expertise. Technologies such as artificial intelligence, data analytics, and cybersecurity are in high demand, and organizations often struggle to find candidates with these niche skills. To address this challenge, organizations can partner with educational institutions, provide upskilling and reskilling opportunities for existing employees, or explore global talent markets. For instance, GE Healthcare partnered with universities to establish a talent pipeline of professionals specializing in digital healthcare solutions.

**End notes**

1. Aguirre, E., De Smet, A., & Parsons, R. (2017). Talent Acquisition: The New Priority for Boards. Harvard Business Review. Retrieved from https://hbr.org/2017/07/talent-acquisition-the-new-priority-for-boards

2. Bersin, J. (2018). Introduction to Talent Acquisition: Three Essential Strategies. Forbes. Retrieved from https://www.forbes.com/sites/joshbersin/2018/01/29/introduction-to-talent-acquisition-three-essential-strategies/#3796623114a8

3. Vaiman, V., Haslberger, A., & Vance, C. M. (2020). "Recognizing the Importance of International Talent Acquisition: A Critical Review." Human Resource Management Review, 30(3), 100672.

4. Cascio, W. (2019). The Importance of Talent Acquisition. Society for Human Resource Management. Retrieved from https://www.shrm.org/resourcesandtools/hr-topics/talent-acquisition/pages/importance-of-talent-acquisition.aspx

5. Chapman, D. S., Uggerslev, K. L., Carroll, S. A., Piasentin, K. A., & Jones, D. A. (2021). "Applicant Attraction to Organizations and Job Choice: A Meta-Analytic Review of the Correlates of Recruiting Outcomes." Journal of Applied Psychology, 90(5), 928-944.

6. Collings, D. G., & Mellahi, K. (2019). "Strategic Talent Management: A Review and Research Agenda." Human Resource Management Review, 19(4), 304-313.

7. Boudreau, J. W., & Cascio, W. F. (2021). "Talent Management: Implications for Organizational Success." Annual Review of Organizational Psychology and Organizational Behavior, 8, 19-41.

8. Garg, P. (2019). Talent Acquisition: Trends, Strategies, and Challenges. Academy of Strategic Management Journal, 18(5), 1-7. Retrieved from https://www.abacademies.org/articles/talent-acquisition-trends-strategies-and-challenges.pdf

9. Kaufman, B. E., & Miller, L. (2020). "The Challenges of Talent Acquisition in a Tight Labor Market." Journal of Labor Research, 41(2), 89-102.

10. Froehlich, D. E., Beausaert, S., & Segers, M. (2021). "Great Expectations: The Role of Psychological Contracts in Shaping the Impact of Continuing Professional Development." European Journal of Training and Development, 45(3), 283-297.

11. Koch, T., Gerber, C., & de Klerk, J. J. (2021). "The Impact of Social Media on Recruitment: Are You LinkedIn?" South African Journal of Human Resource Management, 19, 1-9.

12. Sambamurthy, V. (2018). Digital Transformation: Talent Acquisition Challenges and the Road Ahead. Cutter Business Technology Journal, 31(10), 41-46. Retrieved from https://www.cutter.com/article/digital-transformation-talent-acquisition-challenges-and-road-ahead-500586

13. Society for Human Resource Management. (2016). Talent Acquisition: Understanding the Basics. SHRM. Retrieved from https://www.shrm.org/resourcesandtools/hr-topics/talent-acquisition/pages/understanding-the-basics-of-hr-talent-acquisition.aspx

# Chapter 2:
# Developing a Strategic Recruitment Framework

*"A strategic recruitment framework is the backbone of a successful talent acquisition strategy. It helps you identify, attract, and retain top talent in a competitive market." – Sarah Johnson, senior recruitment advisor*

In today's ever-changing and fast-paced business world, recruitment has been found to be one of the key elements of a successful business. If gotten right, it means the business or organization will continue to strive, expand, and meet its objectives and goals. And if it is not done right, the result will be catastrophic. Even though this aspect of business is very crucial, most people still downplay its importance. If we were to head to the street and ask people what recruitment means to them, you would be surprised at some answers you would get. I can remember a few years ago—to be precise, two years ago—I had a survey on a particular topic that was HR-related, and I asked people their perspective on recruitment. The majority of them held the conception that recruitment was all about filling a vacancy for job placement, beginning with job postings and ending with the issuance of offer letters. Even though it might be right if you look at it from a myopic perspective, The reality is far more complex and nuanced than what this simplistic view suggests. For recruitment to be successful, it has to follow a strategic framework, which means there are lots of things involved, processes, and stages. A strategic recruitment framework provides a systematic approach to identify, attract, evaluate, and select the best candidates for successful talent acquisition. It not only helps organizations find the right people for the right positions but also aligns recruitment efforts with overall business objectives.

A robust recruitment strategy involves a thorough understanding of the organization's current recruitment processes, the number of existing employees, and effective strategies for attracting potential candidates through recruitment marketing. It also includes defining the employee value proposition and allocating a budget for recruitment activities. Additionally, it outlines the criteria and framework for candidate evaluation and selection, as well as the utilization of appropriate software or tools.

While a compact recruitment framework and strategy can envelop the whole recruitment process, it is still very much advisable for companies to adopt a flexible approach in terms of developing specific strategies for each segment of the process. A good example is improving their sourcing strategies to bolster their hiring efforts. This will enable them to tailor their recruitment strategies in such a way that they align with their organizational goals and objectives. For example, if an organization notices that it is experiencing high turnover rates, it can tweak its strategies in such a way that it addresses the issue. However, it is essential that these strategies remain consistent with the overall objectives and values of the company.

# Aligning Recruitment Strategy with Organizational Goals

I have always believed that the best recruitment strategy is the one that aligns with your organizational goals and objectives. There should be a synergy between the two. This is the secret of most successful organizations, especially those that have been in business for decades. When the goals and objectives of the company are clearly defined, it becomes easy to work towards their realization, and one way to effectively do that is by acquiring a workforce with qualified individuals that can seamlessly translate these organizational goals into achievable results. So, in this section, we shall be discussing some of the practical ways of aligning recruitment strategy with organizational goals.

## Understanding organizational goals:

The fact is, for you to have a robust recruitment strategy that aligns with the organizational goals, you must have a clear understanding of what the organization's goals, objectives, and long-term vision are. Every organization has myriads of goals and long-term objectives, such as scaling up their revenue, market expansion, cost reduction, maintaining competitive advantage, innovation, retaining top talents, and so on. Through effective recruitment, organizations can attract individuals who possess the skills, knowledge, and mindset necessary to contribute to the realization of these goals.

## Identify key competencies and skills.

I believe that before recruitment strategies can align organizational goals and objectives, it is very pertinent that the key competencies and skills required for achieving such goals be identified. This can be done by conducting a comprehensive analysis of the future needs and current workforce of the organization. HR departments can collaborate with department managers and executives to determine the skills and competencies necessary for success in each role. By understanding these key competencies, it will be easy for recruitment efforts to be geared towards attracting individuals with the required skill sets.

## Develop a comprehensive job description:

I was talking with my friends during a hangout, and we were discussing what HR managers and recruiters can do differently to make hiring a seamless exercise. At the end of the discussion, his last statement stuck with me: ''A well-crafted job description is a very powerful recruitment tool. A well-defined job description helps prospective employees have a good understanding of the role, responsibilities, and expectations, thereby eliminating any form of confusion''. So, in essence, aligning the job description with the organizational goals, both long-term and short-term, makes it very easy to attract the right type of candidate with the requisite skills and expertise. In addition to that, a well-crafted and detailed job description can help filter out the wrong candidates who are not suitable for the job. This enables the organization to save time and resources that can be invested in hiring individuals who align with the organization's goals.

## Developing Employer Branding Strategies:

I am a HR consultant who has worked and consulted for organizations across different fields. I strongly believe that a strong and vibrant employer brand is very crucial in attracting qualified candidates in our contemporary, competitive job market. Every organization that is serious about attracting top talent should invest in developing strategic employer branding. employer branding that highlights their unique culture, policies, values, and, most importantly, employee value proposition (EVP). EVP in this context can mean showcasing employee testimonials, both past and present, and highlighting career development opportunities.

## Emphasize cultural fit in recruitment.

Aligning recruitment strategy with organizational goals also involves considering cultural fit. Organizations have unique values, beliefs, and work environments. Hiring individuals who align with the organization's culture can positively impact productivity, teamwork, and employee satisfaction. During the recruitment process, it is essential to assess candidates for their cultural fit through interviews, personality assessments, and reference checks. By prioritizing cultural fit, organizations can build a cohesive team that shares the same vision and values, contributing to the overall success of the organization.

## Utilize targeted sourcing strategies.

To align your recruitment strategy with your company goals and objectives, it is pertinent that you maximize targeted sourcing strategies. You can use the traditional methods of recruitment, such as job postings and employment agencies. But the fact is that these traditional methods of recruitment are becoming obsolete and may not attract your ideal candidates. Which is why I always advise companies to leverage various online platforms, professional networks, and industry-specific forums to reach their target prospects who possess the required competencies. By utilizing and maximizing these platforms, organizations can easily attract the right talent that can understand and align with their goals.

## Identifying Target Candidate Profiles:

To be able to attract and hire the right individuals, organizations will need to identify the profiles of candidates they need. This process usually involves outlining the skills, experience, qualifications, expertise, values, and characteristics needed to succeed in the various roles within the organization. By clearly defining the profiles of their ideal talents, HR managers and recruitment specialists can narrow their sourcing and screening efforts to identify candidates that match these criteria.

## Implement strategic interview processes:

The hiring and recruitment process can never be completed without interviews, which goes to show how important they are. Implementing a strategic interview process simply means having a well-structured interview that can enable an organization to access candidates' suitability for the roles. While crafting interview questions, it is pertinent to not only focus on technical skills and abilities but also on evaluating a candidate's alignment with organizational goals. Asking behavioural questions can give HR managers and recruiters insights into how a candidate approached challenging issues in the past and how they may contribute to achieving the organization's objectives.

## Establishing Evaluation and Feedback Mechanisms:

Establishing evaluation and strategic feedback mechanisms is crucial for refining the recruitment and hiring process. In all organizations I have worked with, I always ensure that they establish effective mechanisms for collecting feedback from recruiters, candidates, and other important stakeholders in the hiring process to enable them to pinpoint areas for improvement. The feedback can inform adjustments to recruitment processes and tools in order to meet the organization's evolving needs.

## Monitoring and Measuring Recruitment Metrics:

To gauge how effective their recruitment efforts are, I sincerely urge organizations to ensure that they regularly monitor and measure their recruitment metrics. These may include quality-of-hire, time-to-fill, candidate satisfaction, diversity and inclusion metrics, and other key factors. Tracking and measuring these metrics over time helps companies identify and pin-point trends, benchmark performance against industry standards, and also make data-driven decisions that can help optimize their recruitment and hiring strategies.

# Identifying and assessing talent needs and staff requirements

Let's assume your organization runs a digital marketing agency, and most of your clients are from Latin America and are mostly in the hospitality business. There is a need to hire a direct response content writer who can help create awareness for your brand and that of your clients in order to attract their target audience. It will be catastrophic to hire a novelist who has no knowledge or idea of how to write a sales copy.

Yes, even though he is a writer, his capabilities and skills are not required by your organization and do not also align with your organization's goals and objectives of creating awareness for your clients. This illustration sums up, in a nutshell, what talent needs are all about. Talent needs can be defined as those specific skills, expertise, and capabilities that are needed by an organization in order to attain its strategic objective. So, accessing these talent needs simply means adopting a comprehensive approach towards understanding the skills, knowledge, and capabilities that are required by an organization in order to realize its strategic objectives.

These talent needs vary depending on components such as organizational objectives, both short- and long-term, market trends, type of industry, and even technological advancements. So, identifying them would require assessing current capabilities, anticipating future challenges and opportunities, and determining the types of skills and competencies necessary to address them effectively. This will enable organizations and businesses to recruit, develop, and retain the top talents with the capabilities and skills to drive success, innovation, and continual growth.

In my years of experience as a HR consultant, I have come to find out that some organizations often find it difficult to effectively identify and assess talent needs, which poses a challenge to their strategic workforce planning. So, in order to address that, here is a step-by-step guide on how to effectively identify and assess talent needs within your organization:

## 1. Understand organizational goals:
The first step in the process is for you to have a clear-cut understanding of what your organizational goals and objectives are, both short-term and long-term. When you have understood what your organizational goals and objectives are, it will guide you in assessing the talent needs of the organization.

## 2. Conduct a skills assessment:
The second step will be to critically evaluate the current skills and competencies of the existing workforce. This can be achieved by conducting employee surveys, performance reviews, and skill assessments.

### 3. Gap Analysis:

The third step is what I call a gap analysis. And it simply means evaluating and comparing the current skills and competencies of the present workforce with the skills and competencies that are needed by the organization in order to achieve its goals.

### 4. Future forecasting:

This is very important because it has to do with being able to anticipate your future talent needs based on factors such as the industry you operate in, technological and innovative advancements, and the dynamic nature of your business landscape. You need to consider how roles are evolving and the type of skills and expertise your organization will need in the future.

### 5. Consider Diversity and Inclusion:

When assessing your organization's talent needs, you must consider diversity and inclusion factors. You need to ascertain if your organization has the necessary diversity as it relates to the skills, background, expertise, and perspectives needed to foster innovation and creativity.

### 6. Utilize data and analytics:

Utilizing data and analytics to carry out a comprehensive talent needs assessment is very important. Using the workforce data to analyse performance metrics, turnover rates, and demographic information can enable companies and organizations to identify trends and patterns that can help them make informed decisions when it comes to talent management.

### 7. Market Research:

Conducting market research helps HR managers understand the availability of talent in the job market. In addition, it enables them to pinpoint any skill shortages and areas where it may be difficult to recruit talent.

### 8. Feedback Mechanisms:

Establishing a strategic feedback mechanism is highly recommendable because it helps you collect input from your perspective employees as it regards their career and growth aspirations, training needs, and any other area they feel they can contribute more efficiently.

## Building a robust recruitment plan

As a recruiter or hiring manager working for an organization, one of the things that makes your work a bit easier is a solid recruitment plan. Without it, things can get frustrating and overwhelming because you can't possibly manage the whole process, from juggling new job briefs to sourcing for prospective talents, scheduling interviews, and sometimes also coordinating offers for multiple vacancies. And even if, by miracle, you succeed in managing the whole process by yourself, you will definitely burn out.

So, if you do not want to see yourself in this situation where you are worked up, stressed out, and frustrated, you have to critically assess your recruitment planning process. As a HR manager myself, I understand that sometimes we are under intense pressure, multitasking, and trying to meet deadlines, and because of that, we tend to stick to what has always worked in the past. But we have to understand that things are evolving; what might have worked efficiently for you in the last few months could be obsolete today, becoming a hindrance due to the dynamic nature of the work environment.

I know you might be asking, what now becomes the solution? How do we navigate this challenge? The answers to these questions are quite simple: have a robust recruitment plan. A recruitment plan in this context has to do with an intended strategy that HR managers, recruiters, and hiring teams can implement during the hiring and recruitment process. A recruitment plan is a coherent strategy that can help streamline the whole process, giving everyone involved a clear timeline to work with. This will make your work effective and efficient as a recruiter. For line managers, it offers insights into the time it takes to hire and fill a position. Knowing how long a vacancy will be open allows department heads to introduce contingency plans if necessary.

To build a robust recruitment plan, the following are necessary:

**Collect the headcount plan.**

Ask each departmental head or team leader to share the job roles they intend opening and how these roles can support the actualization of their departmental goals and objectives and those of the main organization in general. By doing so, you will have a good knowledge of the roles that need to be filled urgently and the roles that are more flexible.

Review internal and external materials. You can easily use ATS (applicant tracking software) to measure some of your core hiring metrics. There are lots of good ATS's available, such as workable, greenhouse, lever, teamtailor, Jobvite, and Taleo. Depending on your budget, So with this applicant tracking software, you can measure core hiring metrics such as

**Speed**
• Time to hire
• Average time in each interview stage

**Candidate attraction**
• the platform for job advertisements (hires by source)
• Candidates by source
• Offer acceptance rates.

**Cost**
• cost of hiring a prospect
• Estimated cost vs. actual cost

**Quality**
• Net Promoter Score
• prospect performance after hire
• Actual retention rates

## Equity

• Demographic groups of intending prospects (race, gender, age, disability, veteran status, etc.)
• Hires by demographic groups
• Conversion rates on specific jobs by demographic groups

## Ask for feedback.

Ensure you get the necessary feedback from all the stakeholders involved regarding the hiring process.
* Engage all the prospective talents, recent hires, hiring managers, department leaders, and recruitment specialists in an open-ended discussion to get feedback.
*Ask and find out about potential untapped areas.
Have an honest discussion on areas that need improvement.

*Inquire and ask your potential employees what attracted them to the organization.

## Identify opportunities

After you have successfully reviewed all the information, the next step is to look for signs of any contending issues and also areas of potential opportunities. I recommend that you jot down your baseline in each area to enable you to track improvement in real time.
Typically, these opportunities you find will fall across three areas: talent sourcing, employer brand, or new hire onboarding.

## Talent sourcing

Finding talent: You have to ask yourself: Are there untapped opportunities? If yes, how can you find them? What are the mediums, channels, or sources through which you can find them?

## Branding

Branding: Can you sell your company to potential and prospective hires? Is your employee value proposition (EVP) attractive and convincing enough? If not, how can you improve on it?
*Additionally, do your messages and branding have synergy and are cohesive across your career site, crafted emails, and job postings?

*Do you include your employee value proposition (EVP) in all your job postings?
Most importantly, what are prospective hires and talents saying about your organization in surveys and review sites like Glassdoor?

## Develop the headcount plan.

For you to get to this stage, it simply means that you have gotten the context, data, and insights on previous hires, and with that, you can efficiently plan and strategize for the future. And this requires putting more effort into preparation. I have come to believe that the more a company invests time into these exercises, the easier it will be for them to actualize their recruitment goals on time and within a reasonable budget.

## Gain insight into team goals and priorities.

Through my experience as a HR manager, I have understood that employee-driven objectives steer organizational success. So, engage with senior leadership and department heads to discuss and formulate your company's goals for the year. Will the year be one of growth or efficiency? Are there new departments that will be created or earmarked for growth? Sincerely answering these questions will help you and your team align with the leadership on hiring objectives and the message of the organization.

## Budgeting

Budgeting is an essential part of the recruitment plan because, without it, these plans, no matter how effective and strategic, can't be executed. Budgeting covers the financial costs of recruitment and hiring. But before you start budgeting for the recruitment process, it is pertinent that you understand what the hiring needs of the company are. Once the hiring needs of the company have been identified, the next step is to determine the actual cost of recruiting and hiring the individuals that can fill the vacant positions. Furthermore, you have to effectively allocate resources by leveraging cost-effective strategies; this will ensure that the budget is both flexible and scalable at the same time.

## End notes

1. Del Campo, M. A., & Del Campo, C. M. (2017). Developing a strategic recruitment framework: Strategies and tactics for aligning recruitment strategy with organizational goals. Journal of Organizational Psychology, 42(2), 123-139.

2. Burlingham, B. (2014). How to align your recruitment strategy with organizational goals. Harvard Business Review. https://hbr.org/2014/07/how-to-align-your-recruitment-strategy-with-organizational-goals

3. Gowan, M. A., Holmén, M. S., & Vorhees, P. M. (2019). Assessing talent needs and staff requirements: A review of best practices. Journal of Business and Psychology, 34(4), 437-454.

4. Jones, T. D. (2016). Identifying and assessing talent needs in the workplace: A comprehensive guide. London: Routledge.

5. Saks, A. M., & Gruman, J. A. (2018). Strategic recruitment and talent management: Concepts, frameworks, and practices. Cambridge University Press.

6. Lewis, T. C. (2019). Building a robust recruitment plan: Strategies for attracting and selecting top talent. Human Resource Management Review, 29(1), 91-103.

7. Dietz, J. S., & Fragouli, E. (2017). Strategic recruitment planning: An exploratory study on determining recruitment channels in different contexts. International Journal of Manpower, 38(7), 925-939.

8. Cohen, R. L. (2015). Linking recruitment strategies and organizational goals: A case study of a digital marketing firm. International Journal of Human Resource Management, 26(7), 973-990.

9. Ford, J. K., Favi, R. J., & Singh, A. R. (2018). Assessing staff requirements for growth and expansion: Lessons from successful organizations. Journal of Business and Management, 24(3), 34-51.

10. Hoskisson, R. E., Eden, L., Lau, C. M., & Wright, M. (2017). Entrepreneurial talent management: Aligning recruitment strategy with strategic goals. California Management Review, 59(2), 5-23.

11. Kim, S., & Hollensbe, E. C. (2016). Developing a recruitment framework aligned with organizational goals: A case study of a technology startup. Journal of Management, 42(6), 1768-1797.

12. Montero, M., & Ribeiro, J. L. (2015). Best practices for building a robust recruitment plan in the tourism and hospitality industry. Journal of Human Resources in Hospitality & Tourism, 14(1), 47-64.

13. Wilson, B. W., & Cox, D. J. (2014). Strategic recruitment planning in human resource management: A comprehensive approach. Journal of Business & Economics Research, 12(2), 85-94.

14. Jackson, T. L., & Schuler, R. S. (2020). Assessing talent needs and staff requirements for virtual teams: An empirical examination. Journal of Organizational Behavior, 41(3), 235-252.

15. Collings, D. G., & Mellahi, K. (2019). Global talent management and strategic recruitment. In International Human Resource Management (pp. 59-80). Routledge.

16. Anderson, V., Desreumaux, A., & Fischer, J. A. (2017). Building a robust recruitment plan in the digital age: Insights from recruitment agencies. European Journal of Work and Organizational Psychology, 26(2), 221-234.

# Chapter 3: Attracting the Right Talent

*'Finding the right talent requires a blend of strategic marketing, employer branding, and a deep understanding of what top candidates are looking for.' – Karen Smith, Talent Acquisition Manager*

During a coffee meeting with a manufacturer who was into the making of high-end furniture six months ago, he was complaining of low patronage and how his clients, whom he had on retainer, are now shifting towards his competitors. After my investigations and careful research, which involved going to his furniture shops and having an honest discussion with his clients, I found out that the reason he was having low patronage was simply because of a drop in quality. His furniture was no longer exquisite and well-crafted, which was his hallmark and selling point. Probing further, I found out that the reason for the drop in quality was because his experienced, creative, and skilled carpenters have either opened their own furniture business or have started working for another person. The new carpenters he got were finding it difficult to replicate the standards his company was known for. This goes to show how important attracting the right talent is for both business growth and expansion, especially in today's competitive business landscape. No matter who you are and what level you are in business, attracting the right talent is a panacea for success. So whether you are a brand owner, entrepreneur, solopreneur, CEO, or big corporation looking for creative ways to maintain continued growth or even a start-up who is striving to scale, finding the right type of talent with the required skillset, qualifications, and values, along with your organization's goals and objectives, is very important.

Talent acquisition in this current dispensation has gone beyond just advertising and filling open positions; it has taken the trajectory of finding the right and qualified talents who can effortlessly drive productivity, creativity, and innovation. In this digital and dynamic business landscape, any organization that wants to attract qualified talent will have to initiate and implement efficient recruitment practices and an attractive employer brand. For this to be possible, you have to clearly state and understand what your company's values, culture, and objectives are. This knowledge will enable you to craft an appealing employer brand that showcases your organization's positive work environment, growth opportunities, employee benefits, training programs, and anything else that sets it apart from competitors.

Creating an effective recruitment strategy is another key aspect of attracting the right talent. Creating an effective recruitment strategy in this context will have to do with choosing the best channels and mediums for job postings and advertisements. Some of these channels include social media platforms, industry-specific websites, professional networks, and even online job portals. In addition to that, it is also pertinent that you also craft well-detailed job descriptions that specifically outline the requirements and expectations for the job role.

Furthermore, I strongly believe that nurturing strategic relationships with higher educational centres such as universities, colleges, trade schools, and vocational schools is another potent way to tap into the vast and emerging talent pool. Participating in job fairs, internships, and co-op programs allows organizations to identify promising candidates early on and establish a pipeline for potential future hires.

In addition to building good relationships with schools, internal talent attraction is also very crucial. And I think it is one of the best ways to create a positive workplace culture. Once your internal staff knows that the organization has provisions for career advancement opportunities, training programs, compensation, and other benefits packages, it will not only make them give their best, but it will also be very easy for the organization to retain them, especially the top talents. Lastly, attracting the right talent is not a one-off event but a continuous and ongoing process. I always advise my clients to always review and update their recruitment strategies on a regular basis to adapt to the dynamics of the market environment and candidate expectations. Additionally, asking for feedback from current employees will always give you valuable insights into the effectiveness of your recruitment process.

## Crafting an effective employer brand

In the last two decades, there has been an observable shift in how organizations and employers position themselves to attract their prospective employees and top talent. This paradigm shift has resulted in some organizations being able to effortlessly attract their desired candidates with the requisite skills needed to get the job done. Fortunately, this phenomenon has gained so much momentum that both employers and HR executives are investing so much in it because of its usefulness and inherit benefits. For some who are still not aware of it, it is called employer brand. Employer branding, if well understood and utilized, becomes a catalyst for effective talent acquisition and retention. The employer brand encapsulates the opinions and views of individuals, both prospective employees and those working within the organization, as it relates to the identity of the employer. When we talk about employer brand, we should understand that it is mainly concerned with the workplace environment, focusing on variables such as company culture, reputation, values, and the overall employee experience.

At its core, the employer brand represents the essence of what it feels like to be an employee of a particular organization. As defined by recent thought leaders such as Ambler and Barrow (2020), the employer brand encompasses the promises and expectations that an organization communicates to its current and potential employees. What this simply means is that it is the reflection of an organization's values, culture, leadership, and strong commitment to the growth and continuous well-being of its employees. So, it is safe to describe the employer brand as a guiding beacon that transforms an organization into an employer of choice. Because of the nexus that exists between them, it is impossible to discuss effective talent acquisition without also discussing employer branding. In a study conducted by Berthon et al. (2021), it was found that organizations with strong employer brands have a competitive advantage in attracting high-quality candidates. In addition to that, with an appealing employer brand, it becomes very easy for organizations to not only attract their desired candidates, but it also reduces the huge budget that goes into recruitment. With this age of social media, it has become even easier for organizations to use social media platforms to structure their employer brand perceptions and acceptance.

Having explained what employer brand is all about and why every organization should work towards showcasing an attractive employer brand, I believe it is also crucial that we discuss the best methods and strategies that organizations can use to create a robust and attractive employer brand.

## 1. Define Your Employer Value Proposition (EVP):

I strongly believe that this is the first step every serious-minded organization or employer should take in their effort to create an attractive employer brand. EVP is the unique set of benefits and rewards that you offer to employees in exchange for their skills, experience, and commitment. So, start by articulating your organizational structure, strengths, and other important indices that make it a unique place to work. These indices could be in the form of competitive salaries, career development and advancement opportunities, a healthy company culture, work-life balance, and so on. The goal is to make your EVP as authentic as possible and also align it with your organizational values.

## 2. Understand Your Target Audience:

This is also very crucial in your quest to create an appealing employer brand. Understand your target audience in terms of their needs and wants, who they are, and the possible places to find them. Unfortunately, when we talk about target audiences in talent acquisition, most organizations and employers tend to look outside. So, there is a need to correct that impression. Your target audience consists of your potential candidates and your current employees. So, conduct surveys and interviews in order to gain valuable insights into what motivates your target audience and what they also cherish in an employer. The data will help you structure your messages and initiatives in such a way that they can easily resonate with your target audience.

## 3. Showcase Your Company's Culture:

Most prospective employees have similar aspirations. They all want to work for an organization with a positive and robust culture. It gives them a sense of pride. So, what this entails is that your company's culture plays a significant role in shaping your employer's brand. With that being said, it is very important to showcase your mission statement, values, and other unique aspects of your company culture. You can do this using various channels, like social media, your company's websites, and even the mass media. Additionally, you can also encourage your employees to share their testimonies and how it feels to be a worker in your organization.

### 4. Invest in employee development:
The importance of this can never be overemphasized. Nobody wants to work for an organization that doesn't encourage personal growth and development. This is one of the things prospective employees look out for before applying for or accepting a job role. Employees want to work for organizations that invest in their growth and development. One of the viable ways to show that you invest in and encourage your employee's development is by offering training and retraining programs, mentorship classes, and tuition reimbursement to your employees who wish to upskill and boost their careers. Doing these aforementioned things will showcase your continual commitment to enhancing your employees' career development, thereby reinforcing your reputation as an employer of choice.

### 5. Prioritize employee well-being:
We are in the era of work-life balance, with new slogans such as "lazygirljob" gaining momentum. So as an organization that wishes to improve its employer brand in order to attract top talent, you have to take the initiative.
A healthy work-life balance and support for employee well-being are essential components of a strong employer brand. Let your company or organization be known for offering flexible work arrangements, wellness programs, and mental health resources to help your employees thrive both personally and professionally. The truth is, when employees feel supported and valued, they will not only put in their best but will also speak highly of your organization, recommending it to their friends and acquaintances.

### 6. Create engaging content:
Content marketing can be a powerful tool for building your employer's brand. Create engaging content such as blog posts, videos, and podcasts that showcase your company culture, highlight employee success stories, and provide valuable insights into your industry. Share this content across your digital channels to attract the attention of potential candidates and keep your current employees engaged.

### 7. Foster Diversity and Inclusion:
Diversity and inclusiveness have become the hallmarks of today's competitive job market. Diversity and inclusion are not only crucial for creating a positive work environment but also for enhancing your employer's brand. This is why, as an employer or organization, there is a need to foster a culture where everyone feels welcomed, valued, and included, irrespective of their ethnicity, orientation, religion, colour, background, and identity. So always ensure that you actively recruit and promote diversity and inclusion within your organization.

# Leveraging digital channels for talent attraction

We have talked about how to attract the right talent through strategic channels and mediums like job posting sites, ad placements, and even social media platforms. I feel that there is a need to talk more about these social media platforms, blogs, email platforms, and online communities, which have now become digital channels because of the era that we are in, which is the era of digitalization, as many businesses and organizations are looking for creative ways to attract top talents. With traditional means of talent acquisition, such as job advertising in print media, becoming obsolete, businesses and recruitment professionals are now leveraging the power of digital channels in their quest for talent acquisition. When we talk about digital channels, it is not a foreign word or something that we are unfamiliar with. Digital channels, in their broadest sense, can be described as those online platforms and communication channels that enable individuals and businesses to seamlessly connect, share information, and engage with each other. These channels have emerged simply because of the creativity and innovative nature of digital technology. What makes it indispensable is that each of these digital channels provides a distinct value, unique features, and functionalities. At their core, these digital channels enhance the exchange of digital content, information, and communication in various formats. Be it text, images, videos, or even interactive elements, digital channels have now become a reliable and efficient way to create, publish, distribute, and consume content online.

These channels are very important to businesses because of the advantages they offer when it comes to talent attraction and acquisition. They provide a substantial reach, making it very easy for companies to target a diverse pool of candidates from several locations. Compared to traditional methods, which are very limited when it comes to geographical scope, digital channels allow organizations to tap into a global pool of talents. This is particularly favourable to organizations that operate in multiple locations and are seeking specialized skills and talents that might not be easily found in their local labour markets.

In addition to that, leveraging digital channels for talent attraction and acquisition allows companies and employers to have an active and continuous presence in the job market. This is because by continuously posting job openings and interacting with prospective employees, organizations can position themselves as reputable employers, building strong and strategic employer brand recognition. This is very important when it comes to attracting top talent. Through research, it has been found that most top talents prefer working for companies and employers with a positive reputation and high regard for their employees.

Moreover, digital channels provide opportunities for employers and recruiters to flaunt their organizational culture and values, which will, in the long run, build a strong appeal to top talents who align with these values. Digital channels like social media platforms enable organizations to showcase behind-the-scenes insights and testimonials from both present and past employees, as well as other forms of engaging content that gives prospective candidates a sincere glimpse into their work environment. This level of lucidity helps potential employees assess whether the organizational culture aligns with their own personal values, leading to better long-term employee satisfaction and retention.

In addition to these aforementioned benefits, digital channels are also very cost-effective as a medium for attracting top talents. This is especially true when you compare it to the traditional methods of talent attraction, such as print advertising and attending career fairs. Digital channels mostly require very low capital investment, which is very advantageous for small and medium-scale enterprises (SME's) that are mostly plaque with limited budgets. Through digital channels, these SME's can effectively compete for top talent with larger and more financially buoyant organizations. Digital channels also provide the flexibility to target specific demographics or skill sets, resulting in a more targeted and efficient talent attraction strategy.

But nevertheless, leveraging and using these digital channels for talent acquisition can also have its own challenges. You see, because of the vastness and swift speed of digital platforms, organizations are finding it more difficult to stand out in the face of the numerous information and opportunities that are available to job seekers. Because of this challenge, it is now very crucial for organizations to build a strong online presence that is tailored towards their target audience and, in addition to that, ensure that their job postings are appealing to their potential employees.

Another challenge that comes with these digital channels is the possibility of receiving too many applications, which sometimes do not necessarily match the required criteria. Even though these digital channels give companies access to a wider pool of talent, which sometimes also includes unqualified candidates, this can be very overwhelming to recruiters. To address this challenge, it is pertinent for organizations to build an effective and efficient pre-screening mechanism, such as an applicant tracking system (ATS), to trim down the application process and identify the most suitable candidates.

Additionally, I strongly believe that companies should be very careful of probable privacy and security concerns when leveraging digital channels for talent acquisition. In this age of data theft and cybercrime, there is a need for employers and organizations to put in place data protocols that can be used to protect sensitive information. This will help in building and establishing trust with potential employees.

**End notes**

1. American Staffing Association. (2019). "Staffing Industry Trends."

2. Bersin by Deloitte. (2016). "High-Impact Talent Acquisition."

3. Bersin by Deloitte. (2017). "Winning the War for Talent in the Digital Age."

4. CEB, now Gartner. (2017). "Talent Assessment: Seven Practices of Top Performing Organizations."

5. Deloitte. (2017). "Global Human Capital Trends Report."

6. Forbes. (2018). "How to Attract and Retain Top Talent in 2018."

7. Gallup. (2018). "How Millennials Want to Work and Live."

8. Glassdoor Research. (2019). "Why Workers Quit."

9. Harvard Business Review. (2019). "The Key to Successful Recruiting: Think Like a Marketer."

10. Human Capital Institute. (2017). "The State of Talent Management."

11. Indeed. (2020). "Hiring Lab: State of the Labor Market."

12. LinkedIn Talent Solutions. (2020). "Global Talent Trends Report."

13. McKinsey & Company. (2018). "What Matters Most in Recruiting."

14. Monster. (2017). "The 2017 State of Talent Acquisition."

15. PwC. (2017). "Millennials at Work: Reshaping the Workplace."

16. SHRM (Society for Human Resource Management). (2018). "2018 Talent Acquisition Benchmarking Report."

# Chapter 4: Selecting the Best Candidates

*"If you think it's expensive to hire a professional, wait until you hire an amateur."* – *Red Adair, Oil Well Firefighter*

My friend was having a discussion with his mentor over lunch, and as they progressed in their discussion, which mostly centered on how to reach their organizational goals, his mentor asked him a very important question: "What's the most important element of your organization?" He paused for a few seconds, smiled, and said, His employees. Personally, if I were asked the same question, I would have given the same response my friend gave without hesitation. The most crucial and decisive element of any organization is its human capital. You see, every decision, product, and service that is rendered by any organization is handled by its people. You would then agree with me that the presence of the right type of employees in the appropriate roles can determine if the organization is going to be a success or failure. This underscores the paramount importance of meticulously selecting the best employees from the outset.

As important as this notion resonates, the challenges of management, staying ahead of the competition, and meeting looming deadlines sometimes shroud this important wisdom. Nevertheless, it is very pertinent to recognize that, when it comes to the employee selection process, there is no room for mistakes or cutting corners, regardless of any other grave demand.

## Designing an Effective Selection Process:

If an organization must succeed in the area of talent acquisition, designing an effective employee selection process becomes paramount. The employee selection process is an effective and strategic framework used by organizations to onboard suitable and qualified talents into their workforce. Incorporating top talents with the required skills and expertise into vacant positions. The ultimate goal of the employee selection process is to recruit and engage candidates who not only improve the organization's morale but also commit positively to its corporate identity and culture. Going further, I think it is very important that we distinguish between employee selection and recruitment, as each of them constitutes distinct stages of the hiring process. In the context of our discussion, recruitment leads up to selection, while the latter has to do with the careful examination and identification of the most qualified candidates from the available talent pool. Think of the selection process as that vital phase where the recruitment channel is significantly streamlined, leading to the discovery of top-tier hires. In the 21st century, organizations adopt different approaches when it comes to the selection process to meet their individualized recruitment needs. Even though it is commendable, it is also imperative that these organizations record and document their selection process rigorously before commencing hiring exercises. By outlining the necessary steps and also enabling an attractive, appealing, and positive candidate experience, organizations will not only attract qualified candidates but also improve their reputation as an unprejudiced employer within the community.

**How to design an effective employee selection process**

Creating a detailed employee selection process generally encompasses four to seven steps, although the sequence might vary in response to different organizational needs and preferences.

**1.Announcing the job:**
Before announcing any job vacancy, it is very pertinent to delineate the required qualifications for the role. Once this is done, the HR manager can now proceed to advertise the job vacancy using various digital channels and traditional print media. In addition to that, the services of staffing agencies and recruiters can be employed to create a seamless process.

**2. Reviewing Candidate Applications:**

After all, applications, resumes, and cover letters from the prospective candidates have been received. The next line of action is to carefully scrutinize and filter out candidates whose qualifications and resumes do not match the specified requirements. With the current job market trends, I always advise organizations and employers to be a bit flexible in their expectations, making provision for further evaluation of potential candidates.

**3. Conducting Initial Candidate Screening:**

In order to further streamline the hiring process, it is very pertinent to conduct initial candidate screening. These interviews serve to gauge candidates' commitment and suitability for the role, with questions focusing on their motivations and aspirations for choosing the company.

**4. Conducting in-person interviews:**

After conducting candidate screening and narrowing down the pool bracket, the next line of action is to conduct in-person interviews, where you will have the leverage to assess prospective candidates' qualifications, values, norms, principles, and cultural alignment more comprehensively.

In order to maintain a level of consistency and also track progress, an ATS (applicant tracking system) can be used to ensure communication and cultural compatibility within the interview format.

## 5. Making Final Candidate Selection:

After conducting interviews and also getting feedback from other stakeholders involved, the HR manager or employer selects the most suitable candidate for the vacant position. Most times, an additional backup candidate can be identified as a precautionary measure just to ensure a seamless transition during the testing phases, should the need arise.

## 6. Testing the candidate:

This is the phase where successful candidates undergo drug tests, criminal background checks, and even personality assessments. It is important to say that the testing of the candidate should be done with strict adherence to legal regulations.

## Conducting behavioural and competency-based interviews

During your job-hunting days, when you sent applications to different organizations and firms, was there any point in time you were invited for an interview, and you stepped into a room with so much nervousness that it seemed as if the air crackled with anticipation? The interviewers or HR managers are gazing straight at you with questions already prepared, and you know those questions will serve as a gateway to unravelling the true essence of your potential. If you have experienced that, it will give you a better understanding of what I'm going to be discussing, which is the behavioural and competency-based interview model. It is arguably the best model for conducting interviews because of its dynamic approach that goes beyond the traditional methods of hiring.

A behavioural interview is, for me, a combination of theatrical performances of past experiences and the future aspirations of the prospective candidate or employee. This model of conducting interviews traces its origins to the 1970s. The progenitors of this interview model are the industrial psychologists of that era who strongly believed that there is a nexus between past behaviours and future performance, and by carefully studying this nexus, it becomes possible to uncover the intricacies of human potential.

Almost every comment I have read on behavioural-based interviews points to one meaning, irrespective of how it was said. It simply puts the spotlight on the candidates' past behaviours as an indicator of their future performance. In a behavioural-based interview, the objective is to evaluate the prospective employee's ability to handle challenging situations, gauge their problem-solving skills, and ascertain how well they can interact with their fellow employees and superiors effectively.

For you to effectively conduct a behavioural-based interview, it is very pertinent for you, as an interviewer, employer, or HR manager, to pinpoint the key competencies required for the job. These competencies and requirements will also vary in terms of the job role and the industry in which it is situated. An example of these competencies can include communication and leadership skills, adaptability, problem-solving skills, and teamwork. Once you are able to pinpoint what the required competencies are for the job role, it becomes easy to draft a set of behavioural-based questions targeting the specified areas.

Let's say, for example, that you want to assess a prospective employee's problem-solving skills. You can ask him or her this type of question: "Has there been any time in your previous work experience where you encountered a very exigent problem at work? How were you able to approach the situation, and what steps did you take to resolve it?" This type of question will give you insight into the problem-solving skills of the employee.

In addition to that, the utilization of behavioural-based interviews enables objectivity and fairness in the selection process. This level of fairness and objectivity is achieved by asking all the prospective employees the same type of structured questions and using a predetermined standard to evaluate their responses. This helps in eliminating bias while maintaining the trustworthiness and integrity of the hiring process.

On the other hand, competency-based interviews try to assess if the potential candidate has the specific skills, knowledge, abilities, attributes, and expertise that are directly needed to excel in the vacant role. These competencies, depending on the role, also include technical and bureaucratic expertise, leadership prowess, and a level of creativity and innovation. One of the reasons this interview model has gained popularity is its structure, which enables potential candidates to showcase their abilities by providing insights into how they have applied their proficiency in the required competencies. As a HR manager or recruiter who wants to adopt this interview model, one of the important things you must do is identify the core competencies that are needed in the role. To achieve this, you can consult with the current employees, supervisors, and any other stakeholder in the organization who can provide valuable information regarding the necessary competencies for the vacant position. Once you have been able to pinpoint what these competencies are, you can now structure your interview questions in such a way that it will allow you to measure the candidates' qualifications and abilities and how they fit into those job roles.

For example, if the job role that is being advertised for needs someone with very strong leadership skills and experience, during the interview session with prospective candidates, you can ask them questions like, "Have you ever been in a situation that required you to take charge, lead, and direct a team towards a common goal? If yes, can you describe the strategies you employed and the outcome they achieved?" You see, by asking this type of question, you are allowing the candidate to flaunt their leadership skills through real examples from their past experience.

Both behavioural and competency-based interviews provide valuable insights into a candidate's suitability for a role. However, if you want to strategically utilize these interview models, it is very pertinent for an interviewer, recruiter, or HR manager to ask open-ended questions, and the reason for this is that it gives the candidates the opportunity to give detailed answers. In addition to that, ensure that these questions are focused on the specific competencies that are required for the job role and should be structured in such a manner that enables candidates to elucidate their actions, thoughts, and outcomes in various situations. Going further, another important factor to consider when making use of these types of interview models is active listening. What this means is that as an interviewer, you are expected to pay close attention to the candidate's responses and also follow them up with questions that will make them more open about their experiences. The whole aim of doing these is to be able to obtain an extensive understanding of the skills, values, expertise, experiences, and capabilities of the candidates, which will help you make an informed decision in your hiring process. Aside from skills and competencies, it is also very important that you check if the prospective candidate's values and goals align with those of your organization. Are they culturally fit to work for the organization? These are all things you should also take into consideration.

Furthermore, because of the complexities and technicalities involved in conducting behavioural and competency-based interviews, it is very pertinent that you provide your HR managers with the adequate training and resources needed. This will better equip them with the necessary skills and expertise needed to gauge responses effectively, pinpoint significant behavioural indicators, and make insightful appraisals of each candidate's qualifications and fitness for the role.

## Leveraging assessment tools for objective evaluation

As a HR manager or recruitment expert, what comes to mind when you hear the word "assessment tools"? Have you ever made use of them, and what have been your experiences with them? Assessment tools are very similar to what we discussed in the behavioural and competency-based interview models. In a broad sense, they are all geared towards the same goal, which is helping organizations pinpoint the right candidates with the required skillsets and expertise that perfectly suit the job role. For a working definition, I can describe assessment tools as different types of instrumentalities and techniques designed in such a way that they can easily capture the different competencies and qualities of a potential employee during the selection and hiring process. In a different way, assessment tools simply help organizations make informed decisions on who to hire. Examples of these assessment tools are aptitude tests, cognitive ability tests, standardized tests, structured interviews, simulations, personality assessments, job-related skills, and a whole lot of other strategically constructed exercises.

**Types of Assessment Tools:**
**Psychometric tests:**
Psychometric tests are assessments that are used to test an individual's cognitive ability, personality traits, and problem-solving skills. An example of a psychometric test includes aptitude tests, numerical reasoning tests, and many more. These types of tests help the recruiter or organization have an in-depth understanding of the candidate's strengths, weaknesses, and behavioural tendencies in order to ascertain if they would be a good fit for the role.

**2. Structured Interviews:**
When it comes to structured interviews, they are more of a planned and deliberate set of questions that are used to gauge the individuals' motivations, experiences, and expertise. To ensure fairness and objectivity while using a structured interview model, it is pertinent that the HR manager or recruiter use standardized evaluation criteria.

**3. Simulations and role-plays:**
Simulations and role-play are very necessary for individuals applying for customer service roles, sales representatives, leadership and management positions, healthcare professionals, and even teaching positions. This type of assessment tool is used to simulate real-world job scenarios, which enables prospective employees to showcase their practical problem-solving skills, decision-making skills, and interpersonal competencies in a controlled environment. In addition to that, it gives the recruiter insight into how the candidates perform under pressure and their ability to adapt to challenging and difficult circumstances.

**4. Assessment Centers:**

This has to do with group discussions, case studies, and presentations developed to assess the prospective employees' leadership and managerial abilities and teamwork skills.

**5. Situational Judgement Tests (SJTs):**

SJTs present candidates with hypothetical scenarios and ask them to choose the most appropriate course of action based on the given information. These tests assess candidates' decision-making skills, judgment, and ethical reasoning, providing valuable insights into their ability to navigate complex situations and uphold organizational values.

**The Role of Assessment Tools:**

**1. Enhancing Objectivity:**
I strongly believe that one of the things that assessment tools do is that they help you, as a recruiter or HR manager, become more objective, which in effect enables you to move away from subjective decision-making in your selection and hiring process. In addition to that, organizations that make use of assessment tools reduce bias while at the same time increasing

integrity and competence, and the reason for this is that they solely depend on objective data to make informed hiring decisions.

## 2. Predicting Job Performance:
When an organization adopts strategically designed assessment tools, it gives them insights into how well a prospective candidate can perform on the job, which is far better than what most traditional interview techniques can offer. These assessment tools are designed and developed using well-detailed and rigorous research and statistical analysis that can easily and efficiently gauge abilities, competencies, traits, and behaviours relevant to the job requirements. So, by making use of these assessment tools, recruiters, HR managers, and organizations can make precise projections about a potential candidate's ability to perform in a given role.

## 3. Identifying Skill Gaps:
This is one of the most important functions of these assessment tools. enable an organization to pinpoint already-existing skill gaps in the candidate pool. And when these skill gaps have been identified, organizations can now strategically plan and implement targeted training and development programs to bridge these gaps and develop talents for future growth.

## Strategies for Effective Utilization:

### 1. Align assessment tools with job requirements:
This is very important, and I always advise organizations and recruiters to make sure that they carry out a comprehensive job analysis in order to pinpoint the needed competencies, skills, behaviours, and attributes that can guarantee success in the role. By syncing assessment tools with the job requirements, organizations can ensure that they gauge the important skills and attributes crucial for job performance.

### 2. Ensure Validity and Reliability:
It is always very important and advisable to make use of assessment tools that exhibit high levels of validity and reliability in order to make precise projections about a candidate's job performance. Validity in this context refers to the ability of the assessment tool to measure and evaluate what it needs to evaluate. While reliability has to do with the level of consistency, precision, and stability of the measurement over time,.

### 3. Provide clear instructions and feedback:
Creating a good feedback mechanism is one of the prerequisites for effective and strategic utilization of assessment tools. I have always been of the opinion that in order to create a positive candidate experience and also improve the integrity of the selection and hiring process, it is pertinent for HR managers and recruiters to implement clear-cut instructions about the assessment tools while at the same time providing constructive feedback to candidates following their assessments. This will go a long way in reducing bias,

strengthening trust, and creating a positive employer brand reputation.

## 4. Train assessors and evaluators:
This might be a hard pill to swallow, but I have actually found out that some recruiters and HR managers do not know how to effectively administer and gauge these assessment tools, which is why appropriate training and retraining should be given to anyone involved in the assessment process, most especially recruiters and HR managers. Giving them the required training will improve their competency and efficiency in analysing assessment results, reducing biases, and making well-founded hiring decisions based on objective evidence.

## 5. Combine Multiple Assessment Methods:
For organizations to have a more informed understanding of the candidates' competencies and potential fit for the job role. Recruiters and HR managers should be able to combine multiple assessment methods, such as interviews, psychometric tests, and even practical exercises. Being able to combine these various assessment tools will enable recruiters and HR managers to corroborate information and make well-articulated assessments of candidates' suitability for the role.

## Endnotes

1. Woods, S. A., Ahmed, S., Nikolaou, I., Costa, A. C., & Anderson, N. R. (2020). Personnel Selection in the Digital Age: A Review of Validity and Applicant Reactions, and Future Research Challenges. European Journal of Work and Organizational Psychology, 29(1), 64-77.

2. Bauer, T. N., & Erdogan, B. (2020). Reactions to Recruitment and Selection. In K. F. Geisinger (Ed.), APA Handbook of Testing and Assessment in Psychology, Vol. 2: Testing and Assessment in Industrial and Organizational Psychology (pp. 95-114). American Psychological Association.

3. Raghavan, M., Barocas, S., Kleinberg, J., & Levy, K. (2020). Mitigating Bias in Algorithmic Hiring: Evaluating Claims and Practices. In Proceedings of the 2020 Conference on Fairness, Accountability, and Transparency (pp. 469-481). ACM.

4. Tarique, I., & Schuler, R. S. (2021). Global Talent Management: Literature Review, Integrative Framework, and Suggestions for Further Research. Journal of World Business, 56(2), 101206.

5. Doverspike, D., Arthur Jr, W., Taylor, E. A., & Carr, L. H. (2021). Conducting Competency-Based Behavioural Interviews: Practical Guidelines for Increasing Validity. Journal of Business and Psychology, 36(3), 515-529. https://doi.org/10.1007/s10869-020-09710-8

6. Hsu, Y. R., & Chen, C. H. (2020). Enhancing the Effectiveness of Competency-Based Interviews: A Systematic Approach. Human Resource Management Review, 30(3), 100707. https://doi.org/10.1016/j.hrmr.2019.100707

7. Klehe, U. C., & Latham, G. P. (2020). Behavioural and Situational Interviewing. In D. S. Ones, N. Anderson, H. K. Sinangil, & C. Viswesvaran (Eds.), The SAGE Handbook of Industrial, Work & Organizational Psychology: Personnel Psychology and Employee Performance (2nd ed., pp. 273-290). SAGE Publications.

8. Campion, M. A., Campion, J. E., & Reider, M. H. (2019). Using Structured Interviews to Improve Interview Reliability, Validity, and Users' Reactions. Personnel Psychology, 72(1), 63-98. https://doi.org/10.1111/peps.12267

9. Derous, E., & De Witte, K. (2021). Designing and Conducting Competency-Based Interviews to Reduce Hiring Discrimination. In R. J. Sternberg (Ed.), Social Intelligence and Nonverbal Communication (pp. 305-319). Springer. https://doi.org/10.1007/978-3-030-73885-9_16

10. Levashina, J., Hartwell, C. J., Morgeson, F. P., & Campion, M. A. (2019). The Structured Employment Interview: Narrative and Quantitative Review of the Research Literature. Personnel Psychology, 72(4), 673-719. https://doi.org/10.1111/peps.12312

11. König, C. J., & Klehe, U. C. (2020). Selection Tools: Developments and Research Needs. Current Directions in Psychological Science, 29(2), 158-164. https://doi.org/10.1177/0963721420905506

12. Ryan, A. M., & Derous, E. (2019). The Challenges and Opportunities of Using Technology-Driven Assessment in Selection. Journal of Personnel Psychology, 18(3), 138-145. https://doi.org/10.1027/1866-5888/a000231

13. Anderson, N., & Caldwell, C. (2018). Talent Assessment Strategies: A Review of Methodologies for the 21st Century. International Journal of Selection and Assessment, 26(4), 213-219. https://doi.org/10.1111/ijsa.12217

14. Woo, S. E., & Tay, L. (2020). Modernizing Validity: Addressing Diversity, Equity, and Inclusion in Psychological Assessment. Industrial and Organizational Psychology, 13(4), 477-482. https://doi.org/10.1017/iop.2020.95

15. Lievens, F., Reeve, C. L., & Heggestad, E. D. (2021). An Examination of Situation Judgment Tests for Entry-Level Hiring: Will They Be a Viable Tool in the Future? Annual Review of Organizational Psychology and Organizational Behavior, 8, 445-470. https://doi.org/10.1146/annurev-orgpsych-012420-091353

# Chapter 5: Employer Value Proposition and Candidate Experience

*'A strong EVP is the magnet that attracts top talent and keeps them engaged for the long term." – Sarah Johnson, Recruitment Specialist'*

*'Candidate experience is the true reflection of your company's values and culture. It begins the moment a candidate first interacts with your brand.' – Emily White, Talent Acquisition Manager*

What is an employer value proposition? These are simply distinct sets of benefits and rewards that are being offered to a prospective employee by an employer in exchange for their skills, expertise, and commitment to the organization. In summary, they are just the attributes that an employer showcases to potential and current employees as what makes them unique and different from other employers.

An effective and strategic employer value proposition is a magnate that not only attracts but also retains top talents. This is because a well-crafted EVP showcases the organization's culture, norms, values, and overall employee experience. The importance of EVP in talent acquisition cannot be overemphasized. Companies that understand this are always miles ahead when it comes to the acquisition of top talent that fits perfectly into their organizational goals and objectives.

## Building a Strong Employer Value Proposition

A comprehensive EVP is a powerful instrument for attracting the best and most qualified candidates. In a competitive and dynamic job market. The effective communication of a company's unique and distinct value proposition enables HR managers and recruiters to pique the interest of top talents and also differentiate their employer brand from their competition. In addition to all that, a strong EVP can also help an organization improve its candidate conversion rates, reduce time-to-fill positions, and reduce employee turnover, thereby lowering excessive recruitment costs. So, you can see the important role EVP plays in enhancing employee experience and actualizing organizational goals and objectives. Now that I have briefly explained the importance of employee value propositions (EVP) regarding talent acquisition and retention, it is important that we discuss how to build an effective EVP and the key components involved.

For an organization to build an effective employee value proposition, the following is required:

## 1. Research and Analysis:

To build an effective EVP, efforts and resources must be geared towards research and analysis. This is to analyse and better understand the preferences, choices, motivation, inspiration, and needs of both current and prospective employees. To be able to conduct good research and analysis, I highly recommend that organizations make use of surveys, focus groups, interviews, and even employee feedback mechanisms in order to pinpoint areas for improvement.

## 2. Alignment with organizational values:

This is where most organizations and employers make costly mistakes. Even though you want to attract and retain the best talents in the job market by convincing them that you acknowledge their interest and are willing to offer the best incentives, you should most importantly ensure that your value proposition to them perfectly aligns with your organizational core values, goals, and strategic objectives, both in the short run and long run. This is because your authenticity and consistency as an organization are paramount to building trust and credibility among employees and prospective candidates.

## 3. Communication and branding:

In my years as a HR manager and consultant, I've yet to see any organization that was able to craft a compelling employee value proposition without effective communication and strategic branding. This goes to show you how important these two variables are. As an employer, you can effectively communicate your EVP through various mediums, such as your official website, social media platforms like LinkedIn, recruitment materials, and even through your present employees. In addition to that, you can also make use of compelling and engaging storytelling techniques to present your EVP, showcasing your company's distinct identity and offerings.

## 4. Employee Testimonials and Case Studies:

Adopting employee testimonials and case studies has to do with using real-life experiences, including the success stories of your former and current employees, to build concrete evidence of your EVP in action. You see, testimonials and case studies will always serve as very potent endorsements that will resonate with your prospective employees who are seeking authentic validation of your company's claims.

## 5. Continuous Evaluation and Adaptation:

You have to understand that EVP is an evolving and dynamic concept that reacts to employee feedback and changing market dynamics. Because of this, it is pertinent that you periodically gauge the efficacy of your EVP through employee surveys, retention rates, and other recruitment metrics.

## Key Components of an Effective EVP

### 1. Compelling Vision and Mission:
This is one of the most important components of an EVP. As an employer who wishes to attract top candidates, your EVP should have a clear and compelling vision that effectively communicates your organizational goals, objectives, proposals, and directions. This will go a long way toward infusing a positive spirit and a sense of belonging among your employees.

### 2. Attractive Compensation and Benefits:
For your EVP to be compelling enough to attract top talents and sway them from your competitors, it must include attractive wages and other benefits such as healthcare insurance, retirement plans, and even well-being programs that can significantly enhance the EVP. Additionally, perks such as flexible work arrangements and generous vacation policies cater to the evolving needs of today's workforce.

### 3. Culture and Work Environment:
Another key component of an effective and strategic EVP is a positive work environment that adopts a culture of transparency, integrity, inclusiveness, and collaboration. Employees will also prefer to work where they are valued, respected, and allowed to be creative and innovative.

### 4. Career Growth and Development:
Career growth and development opportunities are crucial components of EVP. Your potential employees want to be sure that you, as an employer, will continuously invest in their individual growth and advancement. Giving them such assurance will not only foster loyalty but will also guarantee their long-term commitment.

### 5. Recognition and Rewards:
Everyone loves to be recognized and appreciated, especially when they have put in their best to actualize a goal. So, adding recognition and rewards as part of your EVP shows that your organization values individual efforts and also reinforces your culture of appreciation and acknowledgement of top performance.

# Creating ideal candidate profiles

Before we start discussing how to create an ideal candidate profile, I feel it is pertinent to understand its importance in the realm of talent acquisition and recruitment. When we talk about an ideal candidate profile, we are simply referring to those relevant attributes that a prospective employee should possess, such as skills, experience, education, background, and expertise, that are in sync with the requirements and culture of the organization. They mostly vary according to the type of organization and the role involved. An ideal candidate profile acts as a compass for HR managers, employers, and recruiters, guiding them in their quest to find the most qualified candidates for the role. Furthermore, an ideal candidate profile helps streamline the process by outlining the qualifications and attributes that are needed to succeed in the role. This helps recruiters target only candidates who possess the required combination of both skills and experiences. Moreover, an ideal candidate profile helps to sync hiring decisions with organizational goals and values. In addition to that, a well-tailored candidate profile helps establish a positive employer brand. This is because when a company effectively communicates what skills, attributes, and values it needs from a candidate, it becomes more appealing to those prospective candidates who align with these expectations.

## Components of an Ideal Candidate Profile

To be able to create an ideal candidate profile, there has to be a comprehensive analysis of the role and its requirements. Although these components may vary in terms of the role involved and the type of organization, some common elements include:

### 1.Job Title and Overview:

This is actually the first piece of information that is expected to be seen in an ideal candidate profile. The job title and overview should provide such information as key responsibilities and objectives needed for the job. This will set the tone for understanding the purpose of the job and the required skills and attributes needed to fulfil it.

### 2. Educational Background:

After clearly stating the job title and overview, the next thing you should do is specify the academic and educational requirements for the role. Does the job require someone with a degree, higher qualifications, or specialized training?

### 3. Relevant Work Experience:

This is where you will specifically state your desired level of experience in terms of the number of working years and any other roles such a prospective candidate should have held. This will enable HR managers and recruitment experts to identify top talents who have displayed competence while working in similar roles in the past

## 4. Technical Skills:

Most jobs require a high level of technical skills to execute, so first of all, ascertain if the job requires technical skills and then identify the types of technical skills and competencies that are needed to excel in such a role. Such technical competencies can include expertise in some software, programming languages, AI tools, and many more. You have to be very specific when it comes to the technical competencies needed to effectively perform the job tasks.

## 5. Soft Skills and Personal Attributes:

This is where you consider essential soft skills and personal attributes that are crucial for the job. Some of these soft skills and personal attributes include communication skills, emotional intelligence, adaptability, teamwork, problem-solving, time management, leadership, creativity, resilience, and integrity. These attributes can also contribute to an employee's overall fit within the organization.

## 6. Cultural Fit:

Cultural fit simply has to do with the company's culture, norms, and values. So, assess the candidates to know if their values align with those of the company. This will help you know if such a candidate would thrive within the company.

## 7. Career Goals and Motivations:

Understanding each prospective candidate's ambitions, motivations, and career goals and aligning them with opportunities offered by your company is very important because it will allow you to pinpoint candidates who are not only qualified for the job role but are also willing to commit to long-term growth and progress within the company.

## Strategies for Creating an Ideal Candidate Profile

To be able to create an ideal candidate profile, it would require the collaborative efforts of both employers, HR managers, recruitment experts, and other important stakeholders within the company. In order to create the ideal candidate profile, here are a few strategies I would want you to consider.

## 1. Conduct a job analysis:

You have to first understand the skills, expertise, and responsibilities required for the job role, which is why it is very pertinent to carry out a detailed job analysis. For you to effectively carry out a comprehensive job analysis, you will need to gather insights from current employees, subject matter experts, HR managers, and other key stakeholders in order to gain a comprehensive understanding of what it means and takes to succeed in such a position.

## 2. Define success metrics:

What are your criteria for measuring success in the role? It needs to be well defined. The reason why I advise organizations to define their success metrics is because it gives them a yardstick for assessing candidates and also ensures that the hiring decisions are in sync with the strategic priorities and objectives of the organization.

## Endnotes

1. Backhaus, K., & Tikoo, S. (2004). Conceptualizing and researching employer branding. Career Development International, 9(5), 501-517.

2. Brettel, M., & Spillner, C. (2016). Employer attractiveness and the role of social media: Implications for employer branding. Journal of Business and Media Psychology, 7(1), 47-64.

3. Cable, D. M., & Turban, D. B. (2003). The value of organizational reputation in the recruitment context: A brand-equity perspective. Journal of Applied Social Psychology, 33(11), 2244-2266.

4. Collett, M. S., & Ewing, M. T. (2007). Employer branding and the employee-brand contract. The International Journal of Organizational Analysis, 15(2), 175-190.

5. Edwards, M. R., Kaul, A., Tsai, C. C., & Thornton, G. C. (2010). Optimal packaging of the employment relationship: Employer branding and labor market segmentation. Organizational Behavior and Human Decision Processes, 112(2), 45-61.

6. Elving, W. J. (2005). The role of communication in organisational change. Corporate Communications: An International Journal, 10(2), 129-138.

7. Ewing, M. T., Pitt, L. F., & De Bussy, N. M. (2002). A longitudinal investigation into the impact of corporate branding on perceived quality. Journal of Product & Brand Management, 11(6), 363-376.

8. Farndale, E., Van Ruiten, J., & Kelliher, C. (2011). The employer brand: A strategic kink in the integrated talent management process. Journal of World Business, 46(1), 50-57.

9. Fasoli, A., Paladino, M. P., & Carnaghi, A. (2017). Candidate–organization strategy fit: The interactive role of values and human capital resources. Frontiers in Psychology, 8, 1347.

10. Graumann, M., Herrmann, P., & Ozimec, A. (2017). Employer brand strength: Individual and organizational determinants. Journal of Applied Social Psychology, 47(3), 131-143.

11. Gürhan-Canli, Z., Hayran, C., & Sarial-Abi, G. (2016). Toward an integrative framework of corporate brand promise. Journal of Marketing, 80(2), 46-66.

12. Highhouse, S., Lievens, F., & Sinar, E. F. (2003). Measuring attraction to organizations. Educational and Psychological Measurement, 63(6), 986-1001.

13. Howard, M. C., Hoffman, S. J., & Lusk, D. B. (2018). Employer branding: A strategy for talent management. Journal of Business Strategy, 39(6), 22-31.

# Chapter 6: Leveraging Technology in Talent Acquisition

*"Harnessing technology in talent acquisition isn't about replacing human touch; it's about enhancing efficiency and effectiveness." – Robert Clark, Recruitment Technology Specialist*

Technology is important to man, just as oxygen is. We can't survive a day without breathing, can we? In the same way, technology has become indispensable to man. Technology affects every aspect of life because of the way it has simplified things, making life so easy and stress-free. Talent acquisition has also been enhanced and made more effective through the use of technology, especially in today's competitive and fast-paced recruitment market. With technologies such as automation, AI, and data analytics apps, it is now much easier for HR managers and recruiters to acquire and retain top talents. This shows the significance and importance of technology in streamlining the talent hiring process. From recruitment to onboarding, performance management, and employee development, technology offers innovative solutions that optimize the entire talent lifecycle. With so many technologies available, the question now becomes: how do organizations, HR managers, and recruiters effectively leverage these technologies in talent acquisition? How can they make use of these technologies to acquire the best candidate for their organization?

## The Role of Artificial Intelligence in Recruitment

AI is one of the technologies that have revolutionized the way things are done. Its impact has been tremendous. In the recruitment scene, it has simplified the hiring process, replacing the traditional approaches to recruitment that were not only time-consuming but also capital-intensive. Although AI cannot replace human involvement in talent acquisition, especially in terms of relationship-building and evaluation of human behavioural skills, it has greatly improved the candidate screening process by providing valuable insights. In addition to that, it has also added the much-needed objectivity and scalability that are important in the hiring process. So, in this section of the book, we shall be discussing extensively the multifaceted role of artificial intelligence in the recruitment process.

## Interview Process:
AI tools have significantly improved the hiring process, making it more effective and efficient. For example, visual assistants are now making use of AI-powered apps to schedule interviews, coordinate, and follow up with potential employees, thereby creating a wholesome candidate experience. Currently, there are many AI-powered video platforms that can easily schedule and conduct structured interviews and evaluate candidate responses, while at the same time providing valuable insights to HR managers and recruiters. This facilitates fairness, integrity, and consistency in the hiring process because of the use of a standardized analysis for all candidates. In addition to that, it is very easy for AI algorithms to pinpoint patterns in interview performance, which will help HR managers and recruiters make better-informed decisions.

## Ethical Considerations:
In the context of what we are discussing, ethical consideration has to do with fair, equal, and respectful treatment of all potential employees during the hiring process. It also hinges on honesty, non-discrimination, transparency, confidentiality, equal opportunities, and compliance. With AI, candidates do not need to worry about personal data breaches or biases during the hiring process.

## Resume Screening:
Resume screening is one of the most tedious things to do as a recruiter or HR manager, and most times, because of the human element involved, there are always issues of bias and errors. This challenge has been effectively solved through the introduction of AI screening tools. These AI tools streamline the process by evaluating resumes against pre-established requirements, thereby eliminating unconscious biases and ensuring a fair evaluation. By prioritizing top candidates based on qualifications and experience, AI accelerates the shortlisting process, allowing recruiters to focus on candidates who best fit the job requirements.

## Predictive Analytics for Candidate Assessment:
With AI-powered predictive analytics, it is now very easy for recruiters to gain valuable insights into potential employee performance and expertise. These AI tools generate these insights by analysing large amounts of data and identifying patterns and correlations that are associated with impressive job performance. This helps employers, HR managers, and recruiters make well-articulated and informed decisions when it comes to identifying the best candidates with the highest potential for success. In addition to that, AI tools can help ascertain if a potential employee will be culturally fit to work for the organization by analysing their social media presence, online behaviour, and other important information.

## Enhancing the Candidate Experience:
AI-powered apps like chatbots improve and enhance the recruitment process through prompt responses to questions and queries made by prospective candidates. In addition to that, it also

offers personalized feedback to these candidates while helping them navigate the application process. Chatbots also make it very easy for prospective candidates to receive updates about their application progress, schedule interviews, and obtain relevant and useful information about the company at any given time. In addition to that, these chatbots can mimic human-like conversations, ensuring a smooth and interactive experience for candidates.

## Utilizing Applicant Tracking Systems (ATS)

One of the most challenging issues HR managers, recruiters, and employers are facing is how to effectively and seamlessly handle the large influx of job applications on their emails once an advertisement has been made for a job opening. This can be attributed to the competitive nature of the job market. This has been a continuous issue until the evolution of the Applicant Tracking System (ATS), which has completely revolutionized and transformed talent acquisition, especially in terms of streamlining the hiring and recruitment process. ATS was introduced as part of the digitalization of the recruitment process, and its effect has been tremendous, especially when it comes to enhancing a company's ability to attract, assess, and hire top-tier talent.

In its simplest terms, an ATS can be described as a technological tool that was developed to systemize and centralize the hiring and recruitment process. Using algorithms and predefined criteria, ATS can seamlessly organize and arrange thousands of applications, making it very easy for HR managers and recruiters to evaluate potential candidates. There are lots of ATSs currently in the digital space, but when it comes to effectiveness, efficiency, and reliability, I would opt for these ones.

1. Workday Recruiting
2. Oracle Taleo
3. Greenhouse
4. iCIMS
5. JazzHR
6. Bullhorn
7. BambooHR
8. ApplicantPro
9. Jobvite
10. Lever
11. CATS Applicant Tracking System
12. SmartRecruiters
13. Recruitee
14. Zoho Recruit
15. Teamtailor
16. Freshteam
17. Newton Applicant Tracking Software
18. PCRecruiter

19. HireHive
20. Breezy HR.


Some of the features of ATS include resume parsing, interview scheduling, applicant ranking, background checks, etc. Because of the different types and brands of ATS, there might be a slight difference in their functionalities, but even at that, there are a few core functionalities that you would find in most ATS, such as resume parsing, which is one of the major functions of an ATS. ATS has algorithms that can easily parse resumes to extract relevant data like work experiences, expertise, skills, and education, saving HR managers the time and stress of manually reviewing so many resumes. Another common functionality of ATS is job posting and distribution. HR managers and recruiters make use of ATS in creating job postings and advertisements. In addition to that, they also use it to distribute these job advertisements across multiple channels and online platforms, increasing the reach of the job advertisements to attract a diverse pool of candidates. Other common functionalities include candidate management, customized workflows, and collaboration tools. The utilization of ATS in talent acquisition and the recruitment process can significantly enhance efficiency, reduce human error, and improve the quality of hires.

Through the digitalization of the application process, ATS completely removes the need for traditional (manual) data entry, lowering the chances of any sort of data vacancy and also saving hours of administrative work. Moreover, with relevant and specific keywords, qualifications, and experiences, an ATS can easily screen applications, ensuring that only suitable prospective candidates advance to the next stage of the hiring process.

In addition to that, ATS has made it easy for organizations to comply with the equal employment opportunity rules. The Applicant Tracking System (ATS) allows HR managers and recruiters to set up uniform criteria for evaluating prospective and potential candidates, thereby reducing the risk of unconscious bias affecting hiring decisions. Further, ATS are known for their ability to secure an applicant's data, protecting sensitive information while at the same time guaranteeing compliance with data protection regulations.


In order to leverage the full potential of ATS for recruitment and hiring, it is pertinent for HR managers, recruiters, companies, and organizations to focus on these strategies. The first strategy is a comprehensive job description. Most importantly, making adequate use of targeted keywords and qualifications within the job posting will help HR managers optimize the ATS screening process in order to recognize candidates that meet the required criteria. In addition to that, organizations can attract a much wider pool of candidates by incorporating ATS into the organization's career website and social media platforms.

Secondly, in order to fully maximize and leverage the full potential and benefits of ATS, it is pertinent that the platform has an intuitive and user-friendly interface that allows prospective candidates to easily navigate the platform and submit their documents. Making the process easy will increase the completion rate, guaranteeing a wider pool for HR managers and employers to assess and find the most qualified candidates for the job.

In addition, adequate and regular training of your HR personnel and recruitment teams on the features and functionalities of ATS and the best way to use them is highly recommended because it will help them effectively leverage the system. Ensuring that your HR and recruitment teams are familiar with the ATS software will also help them customize the search and screening criteria based on the requirements of each job position.

Now we have to understand that even though using an ATS will tremendously enhance the talent acquisition process, there are still a few drawbacks associated with them, and these drawbacks, if not properly handled, can ruin the whole process. One of them is that the software's dependence on keywords for screening, filtering, and organizing resumes may sometimes result in the omission and exemption of qualified candidates. To ratify this issue, I always suggest a periodic review and refining of all the lists of keywords used by the ATS. This will not only optimize the screening process, but it will also reduce the risk of omitting qualified candidates.

**Endnotes**

1. Bersin, J. (2016). The state of talent acquisition: New benchmarks for success. Deloitte University Press.

2. Carrick, J., & Butterfield, R. (2018). The impact of technology on talent acquisition. Journal of Business & Economics Research, 16(3), 105-112.

3. Gartner. (2019). Leverage technology in talent acquisition for improved results. Gartner Research.

4. Green, P. (2020). Talent acquisition technology trends to watch in 2021. Recruiting News Network.

5. Heistor, L., & Walker, H. (2017). From traditional to digital: Transforming talent acquisition. HR Magazine, 62(3), 34-38.

6. Jaaniso, R., & Karras, E. (2018). The role of technology in talent acquisition: A systematic literature review. Computers in Human Behavior, 88, 303-311.

7. Kwon, D. (2019). The impact of artificial intelligence on talent acquisition. Social Science Research Network.

8. Lepak, D. P., & Snell, S. A. (2016). Strategic human resource management: The evolution of the field. Journal of Organizational Effectiveness: People and Performance, 3(2), 127-152.

9. Manci, E. (2020). Leveraging technology in talent acquisition: A guide for HR professionals. Lambert Academic Publishing.

10. Nerad, R., & Heggelund, M. (2020). Innovative recruitment practices for talent acquisition in the digital age. Journal of Innovation & Knowledge, 5(3), 229-237.

11. PwC. (2017). Talent acquisition in a digital world. PwC Research.

12. Resch, M. K., & Daly, K. M. (2018). Leveraging technology to improve human resources management practices. International Journal of Organizational Behavior, 3(2), 13-26.

13. Schiemann, W. A., & Lyle, M. P. (2014). The emerging technology of talent acquisition: Shaping the new world of work. Global Business and Organizational Excellence, 33(1), 43-51.

14. Shanahan, K., & Stevens, M. J. (2016). Talent acquisition in the digital era: Innovation in recruitment and selection. Journal of Business and Psychology, 31(4), 479-486.

15. Society for Human Resource Management. (2018). Leveraging technology in talent acquisition. SHRM Research.

# Chapter 7: Diversity and Inclusion in Recruitment

*"A diverse workforce is a reflection of a changing world and marketplace. Embrace it to stay relevant and competitive." – Sarah Johnson, Recruitment Specialist*

Technology and innovation have made globalization possible, which has made the world a single global village because of the interconnectedness of people. It is no longer surprising to see people of different cultures, nationalities, religions, and races working in the same organization. Because of this trend, the issue of diversity and inclusion has become an important aspect of organizational objectives in terms of maintaining a successful workforce. People want to feel that they belong; they want equity; and they want to know that their efforts are appreciated. And translating it to the workplace means that employees want to have a sense of belonging, and not only that, they want a psychologically safe environment that constantly reassures them of their self-worth, importance, and acceptance. And this is what diversity and inclusion strive to achieve. Nobody is an island; we all need each other to survive. The political scientist would refer to man as a "social animal," meaning there is a constant need for continued interaction. These interactions are needed for our emotional well-being, and if we bring them down to the office environment, these interactions are needed to get things done, find solutions to pressing organizational issues, and also in pursuance of organizational goals and objectives. Now the issue is that the people who initiate these interactions have different personalities, ideas, perspectives, orientations, and experiences. Which can be summed up as individual differences. And where there are individual differences, there will also be a clash of interests. So, the concept of diversity and inclusion makes us aware of these individual differences and the possible ways of addressing them, especially in organizational settings. In the past, when you talked about diversity, what came to mind were simply demographic factors such as gender, ethnicity, race, etc. But due to constant research amid changing trends and the dynamic nature of today's contemporary world, the word diversity now has a much broader meaning, encompassing a wider range of attributes such as sexual orientation, disability status, age, economic and social background, cognitive diversity, and so much more. Because of the recent understanding of the importance of diversity and inclusion (D&I) and its role in organizational success, more organizations recognize that it can be a powerful tool for successful talent acquisition. Diversity and inclusion are now viewed in terms of their multitude of economic and social benefits. So, let's take a look at some of these benefits.

# Benefits of Diversity and Inclusion in the Workforce:

## Enhancing Innovation and Creativity:

One of the unique benefits of having a diversified workforce is that it instils levels of creativity and innovative thinking. This is because the workforce is made up of different people from different cultures, nationalities, and backgrounds, each with their own unique way of thinking, perspectives, experiences, and creativity. Which will further enhance and encourage exploration of novel and unique ideas and approaches. In addition to that, researchers have found that organizations with a diverse workforce are mostly more creative and better equipped to handle complex and difficult issues than organizations with a more homogenous workforce. What this shows is that through a diverse and inclusive workforce, organizations can strategically gain a competitive edge over their competitors in this dynamic and evolving business landscape.

## Improved Decision-making:

An organization with a diverse workforce has a higher probability of making better and more informed decisions because of the insights gained from different people with differing perspectives and thought systems. It is a very well-known and logical fact that when a variety of perspectives are considered, it drastically lowers the risk of groupthink. When diverse teams brainstorm, incorporating a wide range of viewpoints, the end results are mostly well-rounded decisions that are always beneficial to the organization, both in the short and long run.

## Meeting the Needs of Diverse Customers and Markets:

In today's competitive market and diverse consumer base, it is very pertinent and important for organizations to study the needs and wants of their customer demographics in order to offer products and services that can effectively meet these needs. One effective and proven way to get these insights is by employing a workforce that reflects their customer demographics. This will give them very valuable information in terms of cultural perspectives, behaviours, and preferences, thereby empowering them to offer products and services as well as marketing campaigns that resonate with their diverse customer base. In addition to that, research has shown that a diverse and inclusive workforce is better equipped to forecast market trends, recognize emerging opportunities, and adapt to increasing customer demands, which are crucial to organizational success both in the short and long run.

## Fostering a Positive Organizational Culture:

The fact still remains that for any organization to get optimal results from its employees in terms of productivity, creativity, innovation, effectiveness, and efficiency, it must provide an enabling environment that makes its employees feel wanted, acknowledged, and respected. One way to guarantee that is by creating an inclusive workplace culture. When an employee feels wanted, he or she is more likely to be committed and put in their best. In contrast, when organizations neglect to create a diverse and inclusive work environment, the outcome is not favourable to them, as it leads to very high employee turnover and reduced morale and productivity. Furthermore, by prioritizing more diverse and inclusive strategies, organizations can attract and retain top talent, which will give them a competitive edge in this contemporary job market.

**Utilizing Diversity and Inclusion as Strategic Tools for Talent Acquisition:**

Diversity and inclusion, when properly utilized, can be an effective strategy that can improve an organization's talent acquisition process. So, in this section of the book, we shall be discussing how effective diversity and inclusion strategies can be used as an important tool for talent acquisition.

**1. Attracting Top Talent:**

I always advise organizations and firms that wish to attract and retain top and highly skilled talents to make diversity and inclusion their top priorities. This is because prospective employees will always gravitate towards organizations that value diversity and inclusion. The reason for this is simple: there is a strong belief that organizations that prioritize inclusion and diversity are always committed to fairness, equality, and respect.

**2. Expanding the Candidate Pool:**
Organizations that are committed to having a diverse and inclusive workforce will always have a broad candidate pool base because it will afford them the opportunity to have prospective applicants from different backgrounds and demographics, which will be beneficial to the organization in terms of their talent acquisition process by increasing their chances of pinpointing candidates with the required skills and unique perspectives that sync with the organizational goals and objectives.

**3. Enhancing employer brand:**
We have talked about employer brand and how important it is in talent acquisition. One way to improve and enhance your employer brand, making it very attractive and reputable, is by prioritizing diversity and inclusion. When prospective employees know that you are committed to creating a diverse and inclusive work environment, it will bolster your reputation, making your organization the most preferred choice for employees.

**4. Boosting Innovation and Problem-Solving Capabilities:**
When an organizational workforce is made up of people of diverse backgrounds,

perspectives, experiences, and cultures, one of the benefits is that when they brainstorm, it leads to more innovative and insightful ideas and effective solutions. In addition to that, it creates a culture of innovation and adaptability that is necessary for actualizing long-term organizational goals and success.

## Strategies for Attracting Diverse Talent

A few years ago, I had this friend Dennis, a successful entrepreneur and businessman, who owned a reputable start-up company, real estate firms, and a logistics company. He had a successful team filled with creative thinkers who were also go-getters. Dennis wanted to embark on a new business journey that would require him to conquer new frontiers. Being a man with a high business acumen that he has gathered in his two decades of active business life, he knew he needed a team that would reflect a more global community and frontier. So, he called his HR managers and recruitment team, giving them the mandate to rethink their talent acquisition strategies. Dennis had a clear vision of where he was going with his new business approach; he has written down the goals, targets, and objectives of this new business venture, and most importantly, he understands that attracting more diverse talent would not only be beneficial for his new business but would also add new perspectives and valuable insights that can drive innovation and creativity needed to take the business to new heights. This made him embark on a journey with his team to revamp his talent acquisition strategies. This story shows the growing importance organizations and successful entrepreneurs place on the concept of diversity and inclusion. On a daily basis, organizations accept the reality that hiring diverse talent increases their creative and innovative propensity to a whole new level, as well as their overall organizational performance. Research conducted by Mckinsey & Company showed that organizations and firms that have diverse leadership have a higher tendency to outperform their competitors by 21%. This research has once again reaffirmed the fact that nurturing diversity should be a central focus for organizations, HR managers, and recruitment and talent acquisition teams. However, attracting diverse talent requires thoughtful and strategic approaches that go beyond traditional recruitment methods.

To be able to attract diverse talents to your organization, you need to put the following strategies in place:

**Building an Inclusive Employer Brand:**
Employer brands have been discussed in detail because of their key role in talent acquisition. Organizations that want to broaden their scope in terms of attracting diverse talents must be committed to prioritizing inclusivity as part of their employer branding. Efforts should be geared towards effectively communicating inclusion initiatives and policies using various channels and platforms, such as social media, websites, and other employer review platforms. In addition, organizations can leverage storytelling by asking their employees to share stories of their diversity and inclusivity experiences, which can demonstrate a welcoming and

inclusive work environment.

**Crafting Inclusive Job Advertisements:**
When it comes to attracting top talents from different backgrounds, cultures, and experiences, drafting an inclusive job advertisement is very crucial. An inclusive job advertisement would easily resonate with a diverse range of talent. For an inclusive job advertisement to be effective, it must be well-crafted; the language has to be welcoming and inclusive. Certain jargon, languages, phrases, and terminology that are gender sensitive and could segregate certain groups should be avoided; otherwise, the goal of inclusiveness is defeated. Instead, more gender-neutral languages can be adopted. In addition to that, more attention should be placed on crafting clear, concise descriptions of the role advertised, its requirements, and the company culture.

Another important factor to consider when crafting an inclusive job advertisement is how you showcase and highlight diversity within your company. Do you include details regarding your company's initiatives on diversity and your employees' resource groups because they are what will signal that your organization prioritizes inclusion?
For inclusive job advertisements to reach the intended audience, they have to be accessible, which is why accessibility is very important in job advertisements. Accessibility in this context can be in the form of ensuring that the format of the advertisement is accessible to prospective candidates with disabilities by providing substitutes such as assistive technology-friendly formats or video transcripts. Moreover, providing accommodation requests during the application process will also help to showcase a commitment to inclusivity. In order to reach a more diverse talent pool, I highly recommend posting job advertisements on those platforms that are specific to underrepresented professional communities. In addition to that, collaborating with agencies that are geared towards promoting diversity and inclusiveness in related industries can also be an effective strategy for attracting diverse top talents.
Going further, it is very pertinent that this issue be addressed. You have to understand that the goal of crafting an inclusive job advertisement is not limited to only attracting diverse talents. It also encompasses creating a very conducive working environment where all the employees feel included and valued.

**Employee Resource Groups (ERGs)**
I have always maintained that building and nurturing diversity should not stop with recruitment. It should also extend to retaining a diverse workforce. Retention is very vital for organizations that want to achieve long-term success. So, in order to cultivate and maintain this inclusive and diverse working environment, organizations should strive to provide their employees with mentorship programs, employee resource groups (ERG), and training on unconscious bias awareness, among others. These groups provide support and contribute valuable insights to organizational decision-making.

**Diverse Interview Panels:**
This is one effective strategy for attracting diverse talents that most organizations ignore, and the reason is that some of them are yet to grasp its full importance. When an organization makes use of a diverse panel consisting of HR managers and recruitment experts from

different races, backgrounds, and experiences, it not only creates an inclusive and welcoming environment but also demonstrates the organization's dedication to fostering diversity. In addition, it is imperative that the interviewers here are educated and trained on best practices when it comes to diversity and inclusion in order to avoid unintentional biases.

**Footnote**

1. Sharma, G. (2019). Diversity and inclusion in recruitment: Strategies for building a diverse workforce. Journal of Human Resource Management, 21(2), 34-46.

2. Baran, M., & Kłos, M. (2020). Diversity management in the recruitment process: Challenges and best practices. International Journal of Manpower, 41(5), 630-645.

3. Cukier, W., Gagnon, S., Lindo, L. M., Hannan, C. A., & Amato, S. (2021). Diversity and inclusion in the hiring process: A scoping review. International Journal of Human Resource Management, 32(3), 631-664.

4. Alagaraja, M., & Shuck, B. (2022). Fostering inclusive recruitment practices: A qualitative study. Human Resource Development International, 25(1), 97-118.

5. Holgate, J., Kumarappan, L., & Pollert, A. (2019). Ethnic minority communities and employment assistance in austere times: The case of third-sector intermediaries in the UK. Economic and Industrial Democracy, 40(1), 187-207.

6. Sabharwal, M. (2021). Diversity and inclusion in public organizations: Theory, research, and practice. Public Administration Review, 81(3), 402-415.

7. Nguyen, T. T., Felfe, J., & Fooken, I. (2020). Interactive effects of diversity management and diversity climate on job satisfaction and organizational attractiveness. International Journal of Human Resource Management, 31(9), 1180-1208.

8. Prieto, L. C., Phipps, S. T., & Osiri, J. K. (2019). Linking diversity and innovation in organizations: A conceptual framework. Journal of Organizational Culture, Communications and Conflict, 23(1), 1-16.

9. Coetzee, M., & Van Dyk, J. (2022). Diversity management and inclusion practices in the recruitment and selection of employees: A systematic literature review. International Journal of Selection and Assessment, 30(1), 33-50.

10. Azungah, T. (2021). Inclusive recruitment practices for persons with disabilities: Perspectives from Ghana. Personnel Review, 50(1), 238-254.

11. Wittmer, J. L., & Brierton, J. J. (2020). Aligning diversity and inclusion initiatives with recruitment and selection: A conceptual framework. International Journal of Selection and Assessment, 28(1), 46-57.

12. Kell, H. J., Motowidlo, S. J., & Finn, C. A. (2021). Increasing diversity in organizations through inclusive recruitment and selection. Industrial and Organizational Psychology, 14(1), 104-108.

13. Roberson, Q. M. (2019). Diversity in the workplace: A review, synthesis, and future research agenda. Annual Review of Organizational Psychology and Organizational Behavior, 6, 69-88.

14. Chun, J. S., & Cho, K. (2022). Diversity and inclusion in organizations: Past, present, and future. Human Resource Management Review, 32(1), 100762.

15. Kundu, S. C., & Mor, A. (2021). Diversity management practices and organisational attractiveness: Role of Gen Z job seekers. Personnel Review, 50(2), 515-531.

16. Nishii, L. H., & Paluch, R. M. (2021). Leaders as architects of inclusive organizations. Journal of Organizational Behavior, 42(2), 152-171.

17. Olsen, J. E., & Martins, L. L. (2019). Racioethnicity, community makeup, and potential applicants' reactions to organizations' diversity-oriented practices. Journal of Applied Psychology, 104(1), 54-70.

18. Shen, J., Chanda, A., D'Netto, B., & Monga, M. (2019). Managing diversity through human resource management: An international perspective and conceptual framework. The International Journal of Human Resource Management, 20(2), 235-251.

19. Raza, A., Ali, A., Aslam, S., & Zahid, M. (2022). Inclusive diversity management and organizational attractiveness: The mediating role of person-organization fit. Personnel Review, 51(2), 471-490.

20. Triana, M. C., Richard, O. C., & Su, W. (2019). Gender diversity in senior management, strategic change, and firm performance: Examining the mediating nature of strategic change in high tech firms. Research Policy, 48(7), 1672-1682.

# Chapter 8: Nurturing Talent and Employee Retention

*"Nurturing talent means recognizing potential and providing opportunities for growth and advancement within the organization." – Daniel Green, HR Strategist*

Talent nurturing can be said to be one of the overlooked factors that contribute to organizational growth. Because of the fast-paced nature of today's organizational and business landscape, most companies prefer already-made talents that can start producing results immediately after they get employed. The eagerness to meet organizational goals, objectives, and targets, as well as the quest to remain productive, effective, and efficient, has made companies not toe the line of building and nurturing talents. But this is a very wrong move because nurturing and growing talents to gain expertise and experience can be an effective means of employee retention and also building a reputable employer brand. It is a common understanding that I have seen play out over and over again. When you help a prospective candidate with raw potential and enthusiasm groom and nurture their skills until they become professionals, the likelihood of them staying with the organization for an appreciable period is always there.

A good example of an organization that understands the power of nurturing talents and how it contributes to employee retention is Harris Consults, a fast-growing logistics company known for its innovative and client-based services. Recently, Harris Consults had an employee named Maria, a fresh graduate, filled with enthusiasm and eagerness to learn. She is who I would call "raw and unpolished talent." Maria had a knack for app development, and she had a big ambition of making a mark on the world of technology. Immediately after she got employed at Harris Consults as their newest software developer, she felt a sense of belonging, acceptance, and purpose—a sentiment that was also shared by many of her colleagues. And the reason behind this is not far-fetched. At Harris Consults, talent grooming and nurturing were more than just buzzwords. It was a philosophy that was enshrined in the company's culture right from its inception. Maria's growth and success at the firm were tailor-made and carefully crafted, starting from comprehensive on-boarding programs to continuous mentorship and professional development opportunities. One of the effective strategies Harris Consults, adopted towards development was their commitment to continuous learning. Maria has the privilege of accessing different career development resources, such as online courses, mentorship programs, workshops, and conferences, which enabled her to stay abreast of technologies as well as industry trends and practices. In addition to that, the supervisor of her department also encouraged her to obtain certifications and advanced degrees to boost her profile and portfolio. Moreover, the company provides financial incentives and flexible working hours to accommodate the academic pursuits of employees like Maria.

Harris Consults understood perfectly well that talent development is not the only part of the equation; they also acknowledged the importance of employee retention, which is where most companies have failed in this highly competitive job market. So instead of focusing only on the traditional perks and benefits, such as competitive salaries and healthcare packages, Harris Consults adopted a more effective and holistic strategy to ensure employee satisfaction and engagement. The most important aspect of this strategy was the emphasis on work-life balance. This meant that Maria and her colleagues had flexible work scheduling, remote work options for any employee who opted for it, and even allowances during vacations. All these packages were a testament to Harris Consults dedication to endorsing employees' overall well-being. In addition to that, the organization initiated and implemented a culture of appreciation and recognition, regularly celebrating and appreciating each employee's achievement and milestone, irrespective of how big or small it is. But perhaps the most compelling aspect of Harris Consulting's approach to employee retention was its focus on meaningful work. The company encouraged Maria and her colleagues to take the initiative when it comes to brainstorming, contributing innovative ideas, handling projects, and in any other way they deem fit to make a meaningful impact on organizational success. Be it a new product feature or a very complex technical challenge, every project became an avenue and opportunity for career growth and personal fulfilment. As Maria reflected on her journey at Harris Consults, she came to the realization that she stayed with Harris Consults irrespective of other job offers that have been coming her way because of their excellent talent-nurturing strategy. You see, Harris Consulting, through their well-tailored talent nurturing strategy, has not only attracted top talent but has also cultivated a loyal, dedicated workforce ready to take on the challenges of the future.

## Implementing Effective Onboarding Programs

Once you get to this on-boarding stage, it simply means that you have sourced and gotten your top talents for each vacant role, and after you have gone through the processes involved in talent acquisition, the next line of action is to on-board these new hires, which can be a very difficult or easy task depending on how you see it, your level of preparedness, and your intentionality. When I talk about preparedness and intentionality in this context, I'm asking you a direct question on your level of readiness to ensure that these new hires you have acquired are seamlessly integrated into your organizational culture and workflow.

Most new hires have had difficulty settling into their new roles because the management of the organizations that employed them does not have an effective on-boarding process. I recently had a conversation with a friend of mine who just started working with a foodtech company. Initially, he was excited about the opportunity to work for the company, filled with anticipation and enthusiasm as the newest member of the firm. But unfortunately for him, that enthusiasm turned quickly to frustration. He found himself swimming in an ocean of information and data overload while struggling to navigate the complexities associated with his new role. The HR manager and recruiter that interviewed him for the role were not forthcoming on her own end, which means that my friend had no one to ask for clear directions on what to do. This experience is not only peculiar to my friend alone; if you ask around, you might be surprised to know that some of the people you know have also experienced it, as new hires. This goes to show that without a structured and effective on-boarding process, new hires would always find it difficult to settle into their new roles, leading to decreased productivity, a lack of engagement, and increased turnover.

So, what exactly makes an on-boarding program effective? Let's delve into the key components:

First of all, I strongly believe that the first thing to do is to ensure that all paperwork regarding employment has been completed by both parties. Every legal document duly signed, hospital and medical reports and records submitted, letter of appointment issued out, length of employment, work schedule, and everything regarding employee benefits in terms of remuneration, allowances, and health insurance sorted out. After that, the next line of action will be to get the new hires acquainted with their new roles and what will be expected of them. In order to accelerate the process, it is always pertinent for organizations to clearly state their objectives and expectations. As we all know, an effective on-boarding process should start before the new employee's first day at work. So, setting the objectives and expectations before they resume will help in providing the needed clarity for the new hires as it regards their responsibility, task, and performance expectations. In addition to that, the HR manager should ensure that every necessary resource that the new hire needs to get started is duly provided, such as convenient working space, lighting, working materials like laptops and desktops, internet access, desks and chairs, stationery, storage facilities, and so on. Moving forward, the next stage of the on-boarding process should be organizing a well-detailed and structured orientation and integration program for the new hires that will integrate them into the culture, values, goals, mission, and objectives of the organization. Depending on how long the orientation program is expected to last, efforts should be made to introduce the key stakeholders and fellow employees of the organization to the new hires. During the orientation program, the new hires should be educated on the company policies and procedures and how their individual roles fit into the bigger picture.

We also have to look at individual experiences as part of the on-boarding process, especially during the first trimester of the new hire. During this period, it is always important for the organization to provide mentorship support and guidance to the new hires in order to help them navigate the challenging complexities of a new working environment. The reason for this is because these new hires are all unique, with values, culture, norms, and previous working experiences that are peculiar to them. Coming to a new workplace with these attributes can be challenging, especially if they are not in total synchronization with the core values of the company. For example, let's say a new hire came from an organization that allows for group and individual discussion and brainstorming during work hours, and in his current workplace, such behaviours are not condoned. It will definitely take him or her time to adjust to his new office rules and code of conduct. It will be the responsibility of his assigned mentor or supervisor to help him adjust to his or her current work realities. And in order to help him adjust, there should be continuous feedback and support mechanisms. The assigned mentor should offer regular check-ins and feedback sessions in order to know how the new hire is coping with work, find out if he or she is facing any difficulties and challenges, address these challenges, and at the same time celebrate any meaningful progress he makes along the way.

The on-boarding process should not stop at the first month or the first trimester. It should be a long-term process that extends well beyond the initial orientation and integration period. I strongly believe that an effective on-boarding process or program has to include provisions for long-term engagement, such as career development initiatives, performance management systems, and opportunities for advancement within the organization. In addition to that, there should also be regular performance appraisals and evaluations to monitor the employee's performance and offer specialized assistance where needed.

## Developing talent management and succession planning

Now that you have successfully onboarded your new hires and they have become full employees, in my opinion, what you should focus on is how to ensure that these employees give you the expected ROI in terms of productivity, efficiency, creativity, and innovation. That is where talent management comes in. Talent management is not a new concept in the field of human resources; it has to do with establishing a strategic plan and process that enables employees to put in their optimal performance, engagement, and potential to enhance and achieve organizational success. Ideally, talent management is made up of five key steps: planning, attracting, developing, retaining, and transitioning. Once any organization is able to identify these steps and effectively incorporate them, they have solved the puzzle when it comes to talent management. At the core of talent management is the belief that human capital is the most priced and valuable asset of any organization, and because of that, there is a need to continually nurture and develop the skills, potentials, and capabilities of these talents, as well as syncing their individual aims, goals, and performance with the overall organizational strategy. Talent management also involves setting clear expectations, goals, and objectives for employees and providing ongoing feedback and performance evaluations. By ensuring that individual efforts contribute to the larger organizational goals, talent management enhances employee motivation and engagement.

Going further, another important aspect of talent management that is mostly neglected by organizations is the issue of succession planning. When we talk about succession planning, we are simply referring to the ability of an organization to pinpoint thriving employees within the organization with high potential for success and nurture them for key leadership positions. This is to guarantee that there is a seamless transition of leadership roles and positions during events such as employee turnovers, retirements, and sudden vacancies. This action ensures continuity while at the same time reducing the level of disruption that happens when key individuals leave or new roles emerge. You have to understand that disruptions are always bound to happen, but with an effective succession plan, the effect is always minimized. Disruptions happen when employees transition to new roles in the company, or, in some instances, when these employees leave their current company to work for other companies, and also when they retire. If adequate plans are not made for these contingencies, it can lead to structural breakdown within an organization. So, you can agree with me that having a great succession plan is vital for organizational growth. In addition to that, an effective succession plan can also be used to complement an internal mobility program. Currently, we are witnessing lots of lateral career moves because organizations want their employees to have diverse skills and also become multi-faceted. They want employees that can comfortably fit into different roles. For this to be achievable, a strategic succession plan has to be put in place that can systematically assess the leadership pipeline and identify high-potential employees who show the aptitude, skills, and potential to assume critical positions in the future.

So, you see, effective talent management and succession planning are very important to any organization that wants to be successful. Just recently, I heard an interesting story about Mr. Tony, who is the CEO and founder of a thriving footwear company. He has been having growing concerns about his company's ability to maintain steady growth and progress. After consulting with a HR expert, he realized he needed to focus on talent nurturing and the implementation of a strategic succession plan if he wanted to achieve any form of long-term success at Tonystar Inc. He was told by the HR expert that investing in the development and growth of his employees, irrespective of their level and cadre, is a prerequisite for building and sustaining a strong, reliable, and capable workforce.

To start his talent management journey, the first thing Mr. Johnson did was identify who the potential leaders of his enterprise were. To achieve this, he focused on those groups of employees that have exhibited exceptional skills, performance, and a strong alignment with the organizational values, norms, systems, and culture. This group of employees, according to him, were his top talents and could easily fit into any leadership role or position.

After he had successfully identified these top-performing employees with the help of his HR team, the next line of action he undertook was to provide these employees with challenging and difficult assignments, specialized training programs, and most importantly, mentorship from the experienced executives within the organization. In addition to that, he also initiated and implemented cross-functional and cross-departmental collaborations, which exposed these top talents to every aspect of the business.

One such high-potential employee was Mark, who has consistently shown and demonstrated a high level of excellence and leadership abilities for over five years of being with the company. Recognizing his potential, Mr. Tony took a leap of faith by making Mark the leader of a crucial project that had a huge implication on the future of the company, Tonystar Inc. Mark was so appreciative of the opportunity, utilizing it to showcase his great leadership abilities. He led the team with determination, dexterity, innovation, and collaboration. As expected by Mr. Tony, Mark encountered lots of challenges during the course of the project, but he was resolute and persistent, making use of his analytical and problem-solving skills to bring about solutions to the challenges. Moreover, he also sought advice from his mentors and brainstormed with his team to come up with solutions. His dedication, teamwork, and perseverance led to the successful completion of the project in record time.

Seeing the exceptional leadership qualities exhibited by Mark during the course of the project, Mr. Tony was convinced that Mark should be included in the succession planning process. He believed that Mark had the required skills, experience, expertise, and behavioural qualities to take on a much bigger and wider role in the future. As a result of that, Mark was provided with more specialized training and exposure in order to broaden and hone his skills. Because of the ingenuity exhibited by Mark, Mr. Tony and other stakeholders at Tonystar Inc. resolved to continuously invest in talent nurturing, management, and succession planning. They went ahead to draft and establish a holistic and comprehensive performance appraisal system that enabled managers and supervisors to analyse and evaluate an employee's work performance, identifying core areas of strength and progress as well as areas that needed improvement. The data gotten from this comprehensive analysis and evaluation was used to create a well-tailored development plan for the workforce, ensuring that each employee received the required training and support needed to improve their skills and expertise.

This resulted in a tremendous increase in employee satisfaction, retention, and engagement. The employees at Tonystar Inc. felt a sense of belonging because the company and its management recognized and rewarded their potential and expertise. In addition to that, Mr. Tony's company also witnessed seamless transitions during leadership changes because of the availability of ready and qualified candidates waiting to step into key leadership roles.

**footnote**

1. Aguinis, H., & Kraiger, K. (2019). Benefits of training and development for individuals and teams, organizations, and society. Annual Review of Psychology, 60, 451-474.

2. Biswas, S., & Bhatnagar, J. (2021). Talent management and employee engagement as predictors of career satisfaction: A study of Indian IT professionals. Journal of Indian Business Research, 13(1), 76-92.

3. Shuck, B., & Wollard, K. (2020). Employee engagement and HRD: A seminal review of the foundations. Human Resource Development Review, 9(1), 89-110.

4. Lockwood, N. R. (2021). Talent management: Driver for organizational success. SHRM Research Quarterly, 16(4), 1-10.

5. Cappelli, P., & Keller, J. R. (2020). Talent management: Conceptual approaches and practical challenges. Annual Review of Organizational Psychology and Organizational Behavior, 1, 305-331.

6. Dries, N. (2019). The psychology of talent management: A review and research agenda. Human Resource Management Review, 23(4), 272-285.

7. Gallardo-Gallardo, E., Dries, N., & González-Cruz, T. F. (2020). Talent identification in the workplace: A review of the literature. European Journal of Training and Development, 36(1), 26-45.

8. Zickermann, T., & de Lange, P. (2022). Talent management and employee retention: The mediating role of work engagement and perceived supervisor support. The International Journal of Human Resource Management, 33(9), 1878-1909.

9. Dahiya, R., & Rangnekar, S. (2019). Servant leadership, leader-member exchange, and employee creativity: The mediating role of psychological empowerment. Management Research Review, 42(6), 698-719.

10. Mutonyi, B. R., Slåtten, T., & Lien, G. (2020). Empowering leadership, work engagement and intrinsic motivation. Leadership & Organization Development Journal, 41(2), 279-292.

11. Kasemsap, K. (2021). Fostering employee engagement through effective talent management practices. International Journal of Productivity and Performance Management, 70(1), 149-169.

12. Malik, A., Pereira, V., & Budhwar, P. (2022). Talent management practices in global organizations: A review and a research agenda. The International Journal of Human Resource Management, 33(1), 1-30.

13. Anand, S., Vidyarthi, P. R., & Rolnicki, S. (2022). Leader-member exchange and employee creativity: The mediating role of psychological empowerment. The Leadership Quarterly, 29(3), 365-377.

14. Dong, Y., Bartol, K. M., Zhang, Z. X., & Li, C. (2021). Enhancing employee creativity via individual skill development and team knowledge sharing: Influences of dual-focused transformational leadership. Journal of Organizational Behavior, 32(1), 89-104.

# Chapter 9: Future Trends in Talent Acquisition

*"Future-proofing talent acquisition means embracing remote work capabilities and virtual hiring processes to attract a global talent pool." – Olivia Harris, Remote Recruitment Specialist*

The processes and methods of talent acquisition are changing on a daily basis due to new technologies and phenomena. The COVID-19 pandemic came with a whole range of changes that affected almost every aspect of our human endeavours, including how we recruit and hire. Because of the total breakdown of institutions and workflow caused by the global lockdown, organizations, HR managers, recruiters, and other stakeholders in the job market had to come up with an effective contingency plan. In addition to that, the introduction of Gen Z to the job market necessitated a paradigm shift away from the traditional methods of hiring and talent acquisition in order to accommodate their deep-level exposure to innovation, technology, ways of thinking, and approaches. These events and so many more have led to a seismic upheaval that is constantly challenging the traditional and conventional wisdom of talent acquisition and hiring.

In a recent conference organized by HR managers and recruiters that I had the opportunity to attend, the keynote speaker reiterated these same views and even went ahead to expound on them. According to him, "the process and method of hiring and attracting top talents are changing before our eyes; the days of posting job ads on billboards, screens, and print media and having to spend days reading and evaluating piles of resumes are gone. The future of talent acquisition and hiring is now all about organizations positioning themselves to stay ahead of the curve in order to effectively anticipate both the needs of the business and the prospective candidates."

He went further to explain that artificial intelligence (AI) and automation are already at the forefront when it comes to the future of talent acquisition, and I totally agree with him because if you take a closer look at how things are unfolding in the job market, you will begin to appreciate the pivotal role AI is currently playing in the recruitment of top talents. Virtual assistants, which are a form of AI, can easily sift through thousands of applications with precise accuracy, pinpoint the most qualified candidates, and even schedule screening interviews, making the whole recruitment process very easy for HR managers and recruiters.

A friend of mine who runs a hiring agency shared a story of how an AI-powered applicant tracking system revolutionized his agency's hiring process. According to him, "it was a game-changer for us. The system's machine learning algorithms could quickly identify the most promising candidates, freeing up our team to focus on the human aspects of the hiring process."

Now, this does not mean that AI can comfortably replace the human touch when it comes to hiring and recruitment; no matter how efficient these AI tools are, they would still need to be prompted by humans. So, let's just see them as valuable tools when it comes to streamlining and optimizing the hiring process.

Going further, we are witnessing a shift from the traditional aspect of transactional recruitment, which only sees recruitment and hiring as an immediate and direct exchange of services between an organization and a potential employee. This shift is necessitated by the inadequacies that are inherent in this type of recruitment, such as short-term focus, minimal relationship building, limited engagement, and so on. The emphasis is now on a relationship-based type of recruitment that focuses on establishing a long-term relationship and trust with the prospective candidate. Research has shown that this type of recruitment model is a win-win for all parties involved as it improves the employer brand of the company as well as creating a memorable candidate experience for the prospective candidate, especially now that there is a growing importance on candidate experience, which can be attributed to the fact that top talents and highly skilled candidates have more options than ever in today's dynamic job market. This leverage means that organizations and recruiters have to adopt a recruitment process that is not only engaging but also exciting for these candidates. So, it is not just enough to offer competitive salaries and other benefit packages. According to a recent poll conducted on LinkedIn, prospective employees indicated that the candidate experience and how they were treated during the interview stage influenced their decisions to either join a company or not. In addition to that, according to a survey by CareerArc, 72% of job seekers who had a negative experience during the application process shared that experience online or with someone they knew. On the flip side, candidates who had a positive experience were more likely to increase their relationship with the company through social media, even if they didn't get the job. So, you can appreciate the importance of candidate experience in talent acquisition and the reason for its growing importance.

Another trend in talent acquisition that is attracting the right spotlight is the focus on skill-based hiring. The traditional approach of judging a candidate's competence by his or her academic qualification and professional certification is becoming obsolete, so it is safe to say that these days "a degree alone will not get you the job." Just as a recruiter remarked, "what we are currently looking for in candidates are skills, experience, and expertise because we want prospective candidates who can immediately hit the ground running once employed and contribute to the growth of the organization." I had a female friend who just graduated from the university with a BSc in graphics designs; she didn't spend much time before she secured a job as a graphics designer in a marketing agency.

What stood her out from other candidates was her skills and expertise. She has far more to offer than just her academic qualifications; she has honed her skills by working as a freelancer and developing an impressive portfolio of creative work.

## Emerging Technologies and Their Impact on Recruitment

Emerging technologies have been on the lips of every professional, especially in this post-COVID-19 era. The realities of the pandemic have taught us a very big lesson, which is that "technology and innovation" are our only defences against any unexpected occurrence in the future. What this implies is that in every sector and sphere of life, there should be conscious efforts to come up with creative and innovative ways of doing things. In other words, there should be constant technological advancements to cater for the dynamic nature of today's world.

Bringing it down to the area of recruitment, the last couple of years have witnessed a tremendous advancement of technology with respect to how recruitment is being done. This remarkable transformation has revolutionized the recruitment process, making it more candidate-centered and data-driven.

These emerging technologies are changing the recruitment landscape, making it easier for organizations to pinpoint and attract the best and most qualified candidates in a competitive job market. In this section of the book, we shall be exploring the impact of these emerging technologies on the recruitment industry and how they are redefining the way organizations approach talent acquisition.

The first on the list is video interviewing. Video interviewing has emerged as a major technological advancement when it comes to talent acquisition. It has simplified the hiring process by making it more flexible, efficient, and accessible to both the recruiters and the prospective candidates. The fact that video interviewing has to do with remotely conducting job interview sessions via video conferencing platforms such as Zoom, Google Meet, etc. eliminates any form of geographical barrier. In addition to that, it also saves both time and resources for all the parties involved. When you compare video interviewing with traditional in-person interviews that involve scheduling physical meetings, logistics arrangements, and accommodation if the candidate is coming from a faraway place, you will understand why video interviewing has become very pivotal in conducting and achieving a seamless recruitment process.

Furthermore, video interviewing also makes it very easy for recruiters to reach a wide pool of candidates, including those who might not have the privilege and opportunity to be physically present due to distance or any other limitations. Several industries have embraced video interviewing with positive outcomes. For example, in the tech world, reputable companies like Google and Microsoft are known for making use of video interviews when it comes to evaluating prospective employees for technical roles. Fortunately, according to them, this method of conducting interviews has tremendously improved the efficiency of their hiring process, while at the same time helping reduce the cost associated with conducting an in-person interview session.

Additionally, many organizations in the healthcare sector are using video interviewing as a way to streamline their hiring processes, especially for positions that require candidates with specialized skills, experience, and expertise. A very good example are medical centers like Mayo Clinic, which were among the first medical institutions to adopt video interviewing for evaluating prospective employees for nursing and physician roles, enabling them to fill critical positions more rapidly.

Moreover, during the COVID-19 pandemic, video interviewing became essential for maintaining recruitment efforts because of the social distancing guidelines. Many companies have transitioned their entire hiring process online, relying on video interviews to assess candidates remotely.

However, we have to understand that notwithstanding the benefits of video interviewing, there are still myriad challenges associated with it, such as a lack of personal interaction, technical glitches, and even biases in the evaluation of candidates. This challenge, if not dealt with by recruiters and employers, will eventually make the technology ineffective and obsolete.

Going further, another technological advancement that has recently emerged and is changing the face of the recruitment and hiring process is augmented reality (AR) and virtual reality (VR).

These two innovative technologies have greatly impacted the hiring process, revolutionizing the interaction between employers and their prospective employees by creating an intriguing immersive experience.

Augmented reality can be described as a technology that superimposes digital data, such as videos, 3D models, and even images, onto an individual's real-world environment. Relating to recruitment and hiring, augmented reality can be pivotal in improving the prospective candidate's interview experience and, at the same time, simplifying the whole hiring process. One of the reasons for the continuous ascendency of augmented reality in the recruitment process is because it allows prospective employees to immerse themselves in a simulated work environment, making it possible for them to have actual experience and knowledge of the day-to-day tasks, responsibilities, and requirements of their assigned role. The experience is beneficial to both the prospective candidates and the recruiter because it enables the candidates to make insightful decisions about their career choices, and on the other hand, it allows the recruiter to evaluate the candidate's skills and potential in order to ascertain if they are the right fit for the position.

Additionally, another reason why organizations and recruiters are embracing this innovative technology is because it allows them to create virtual hiring events and career fairs. With these virtual hiring events, prospective candidates can easily engage and communicate with company representatives, which most times leads to virtual interview sessions, all from the comfort of their own devices, thereby eliminating distance and any other form of geographical barriers. A typical example of how AR can impact the recruitment and hiring processes of organizations was recorded by Mr. Davis, who is a HR consultant and runs a private HR consulting agency. He and his team were recently contracted to develop a mobile augmented reality (AR) app that enabled prospective employees of a firm to have a virtual tour of the firm's offices, getting a glimpse of the work environment while at the same time having the opportunity to communicate with the present staff and employees of the firm through virtual avatars. This immersive experience enabled the prospective employees to have a genuine and interactive view of the firm's day-to-day activities, values, norms, and culture. Through this AR app that Mr. Davis and his team created, prospective employees took part in virtual job simulations and challenges designed by the firm to evaluate and know if their skills, expertise, and other competencies sync with the job positions they were applying for. This method not only ensured a more accurate evaluation of the candidates by the HR team but also enabled the candidates to display their skills and capabilities in a dynamic and interactive way. Furthermore, the AR application made it very easy and possible for the company's HR team to conduct virtual interview sessions with the candidates irrespective of their current location, saving both the company and prospective candidates time and resources on travel expenses. This allowed them to reach a wider pool of candidates and ensure a more efficient and streamlined hiring process. As a result of implementing AR technology in their recruitment and hiring processes, the firm witnessed an unprecedented increase in the quality of their hires.

On the other hand, virtual reality (VR) takes the whole immersive experience to an entirely new level by developing a computer-generated environment that is completely simulated, allowing the individual to interact with the environment. Relating to the recruitment and hiring process, VR can be used to improve how prospective candidates are evaluated in the sense that it allows candidates to display their skills and expertise in a more captivating way. One of the key applications of VR in recruitment is the use of virtual assessments and simulations. These methods are being used by recruiters during the interview sessions because they make it possible for candidates to showcase their competencies, such as problem-solving abilities, teamwork skills, and decision-making capabilities. All they need to do is simply place these prospective candidates in realistic work scenarios using virtual reality. This process helps recruiters, HR managers, and employers have a thorough comprehension and in-depth knowledge of the candidate's abilities, enabling them to make more informed hiring decisions.

Another emerging technology that is worth talking about is blockchain technology. Its current impact on the recruitment and hiring processes of major organizations and companies has become a thing of interest. For someone reading this who doesn't know what blockchain technology is all about, it is best described as an advanced technology that is made up of a decentralized and distributed digital ledger that has the ability to securely record transactions across multiple computers in a network. It is a technology that is revolutionizing all spheres of human endeavours, including how we recruit and hire our workforce. The major features of blockchain that have made it a force to be reckoned with are that it is decentralized, transparent, immutable, and secure.

Originally, blockchain technology was specifically designed as an underlying technology for Bitcoin, but currently it is being used far beyond the world of cryptocurrencies in industries and sectors such as supply chain management, health, tourism, finance, and recruitment, which is where our interest lies. Blockchain technology has significantly transformed the recruitment and hiring landscape in several ways, such as credential verification. Previously, this was a major issue in the recruitment process because recruiters and companies were having hard times trying to verify the qualifications of their prospective candidates, both in terms of academics and work experience. But with the introduction of blockchain technology, the problem has been solved. Most institutions now have secure and immutable digital records of their students' certifications. A good example of such an institution is MIT. Currently, MIT has their digital diplomas on blockchain, which has made it very easy and convenient for their graduates to directly share their verified certificates with their employers and recruiters. This approach has drastically reduced both the time, cost, effort, and other inconveniences involved in verifying academic and educational certifications. Another way blockchain technology is revolutionizing the recruitment process is in terms of enhanced security and privacy. With this technology, candidates do not need to fear that their sensitive information, like personal data, will be tampered with. Organizations that make use of this technology have a very minimal number of cases of data breaches. Companies like TrustedKey, which is a reliable blockchain-based platform providing services such as secure identity management, allow candidates to control who has access to their personal information. This has made it easy for recruiters to trust the genuineness of the candidate's data and information, reducing the tendency to hire based on deceptive information. Additionally, blockchain technology has also contributed to the growth of remote work by providing easy payment services for international workers. Blockchain companies such as Bitwage have made it very convenient for employees like freelancers, international workers, and remote workers to receive their salaries and bonuses in Bitcoin, thereby reducing the difficulty associated with making international payments. Another blockchain company called HireMatch is helping to simplify the hiring process by directly connecting potential employees (job seekers) with employers using blockchain technology. It rewards users with cryptocurrency tokens for helping match candidates with job openings, leveraging the power of the community to enhance recruitment.

## The Rise of Remote Work and Flexible Talent Acquisition

Remote jobs became a global sensation and trend during the COVID-19 pandemic. The world was forced to adapt to it because of the total lockdown that we witnessed during that period of time. It was as if there was a worldwide retrenchment of workers without an official sack letter. Nobody was on the street, schools were shut down, and the workflow was put to a halt, resulting in economic stagnation and a crisis that has not been witnessed for over a century as major companies quoted revenue losses that amounted to billions of dollars. It was indeed a dilemma that didn't seem to have a solution. This was the testimony of most of the organizations during the early period of the global lockdown. But something had to be done, so the question now became how to get the global workforce back to work without endangering their lives. They couldn't return to an office environment because of social distancing and quarantining. The only reasonable solution was for them to work right from their individual homes; that way, it was safe and convenient for everyone involved. This was meant to be a temporary solution that the world adapted to until a vaccine was produced, but fortunately, what was once seen as a temporary solution soon revealed itself to be a glimpse into a future where flexibility and adaptability would reign supreme. Companies and organizations that rejected the concept of remote work had no choice but to fully embrace it after realizing the perks associated with it, both on the side of the employees and their bottom line.

The post-COVID era witnessed a tremendous shift in the work schedule of many organizations and their employees as the traditional white-collar 9-5 workday began to tilt towards a more flexible and fluid schedule. This also led to the emergence of a new epoch in talent acquisition. Employers and recruiters were no longer limited by any sort of geographical barrier when it came to talent acquisition and recruitment. In addition to that, organizations and employers have enjoyed unlimited access to a global pool of top talents who could contribute to the continuous growth and success of their organizations with their diverse range of skills, expertise, and experience.

Anyone who has taken a closer look at the job market will agree with me that the shift towards remote work settings and flexible talent acquisition has immensely revolutionized the way we work. The fact that employees are not restricted to a physical work environment has enabled them to create a healthy balance between their professional work and personal lives, leading to increased productivity, efficiency, engagement, job satisfaction, and a reduced turnover rate.

Moreover, as more and more organizations are joining the queue and accepting remote work settings and flexible talent acquisition, it has led to a more diverse and inclusive workforce, resulting in more creativity and innovative ideas.

The idea of creating a work-life balance is making more and more people accept this new working method. Young people want to have the freedom to explore and do other exciting things with their lives, such as traveling and networking. They feel that being stuck at the office from morning to evening, Monday to Friday or Saturday, would not avail them of such an opportunity. In addition to that, remote work offers individuals, especially freelancers, the opportunity to work multiple jobs at the same time because they are the ones to fix their work schedule, so allocating the required amount of time to get each job done becomes possible. I have a friend who is a copywriter, digital marketer, and visual assistant. On his busy days, he handles up to 3–5 clients, attends to them, and works on their individual projects, respectively. So, you can see that, from an economic standpoint, remote work settings are beneficial to employees and also employers. We are witnessing a rising trend in organizations, mostly start-ups, outsourcing their employees because it is more cost-effective and convenient. it is now common to see organizations whose workforce is made up of people on hourly, daily, and weekly contracts. They are not fully employed, making it very easy to terminate the contractual agreement whenever the need arises. The need for this type of work arrangement is borne out of the present economic realities that we are facing. Most companies are already downsizing their work force to stay afloat, and those who are not downsizing are looking for creative ways to cut wages. According to Mr. Kingston, who is a HR business partner, "flexible talent acquisition has evolved to the point that it is being used to cater for the dynamic nature of today's organization and also the constantly changing labour market. Most organizations cannot afford to maintain a full traditional workforce, which is why they are utilizing the gig economy, which allows them to hire a freelancer, paying him or her on an hourly basis for a specific amount of money, which in most cases is lower than what they would have paid a full-time employee at the end of the month."

To get a more personalized perspective on the issue of remote work. I conducted an interview where I asked a few people their opinions about the three different types of work settings (remote work settings, hybrid work settings, and on-site work settings). The type they preferred and their reasons for that.

Mrs. Chiwe, a young HR professional, shared her perspective: "Remote work offers flexibility and eliminates commuting, but it can be isolating. Hybrid work combines the best of both worlds, with a mix of remote and in-office work. The traditional 9-5 can provide structure and a clear separation between work and personal life. I prefer hybrid work because it allows me to enjoy the benefits of both."

The allure of remote work is undeniable, especially for young people seeking greater work-life integration. "I can do the work anytime, anywhere," explained Mr. Ebere, a chartered accountant. "It affords me the chance to do other things. One can take 2 or 3 remote jobs at the same time, depending on your capacity, but you cannot say the same for other categories of work."

However, not everyone is convinced that remote work is the panacea. Ms. Chinamerem, a start-up founder and public health practitioner, highlighted the value of the hybrid model: "It all depends on the kind of work, but in general, I would prefer hybrid work. It is a combination of remote work and normal work (9–5). Most importantly, it is flexible, and I also get the opportunity to collaborate with my co-workers."

Barrister Ebere takes a pragmatic approach, stating, "If they all pay the same, remote is better for me. It's more convenient and allows you time to do and focus on other things. With a remote work setting, you can shuffle two to three different jobs comfortably. Even when the pay for a remote job is a bit less, I will choose remote work too, because when you calculate the transportation going to work every day, it might be more expensive than the little difference between remote and full-time (on-site)."

Mr. Fortune, an MSc student and agriculturist, towed the line of hybrid work settings: "Hybrid work gives him the ability to tour and travel to different places and also work from his comfort zone. In addition to that, the pay for most hybrid jobs is always higher when compared to others.

Finally, Ms. Miriam, a sales rep for a pension fund agency, sees a remote job as the best option for her. "I'd choose a remote job. It'd enable me to work from anywhere in the world because I love traveling. I wouldn't have to worry about waking up early every day, preparing for work, and hustling for a seat in the bus each morning.

From these responses, it shows that the traditional 9-5 (on-site) work setting has not fully gone into extinction, although people are favouring the modified fashion, which is the hybrid work setting, the reason being that it has both the attributes and characteristics of the traditional 9-5 work setting and also those of a remote work setting. With the hybrid work settings, you can work from home and still go to the office, so the issues of loneliness and lack of physical interaction, which are among the challenges of working a fully remote job, are eliminated. Moreover, just as Ms. Chinamerem pointed out, hybrid work settings give her the opportunity to collaborate with her co-owners. Whatever she learned at the workplace can be effectively put into practice when she's working at home. Which means there is no skill gap. In conclusion, hybrid and remote work have become the new normal due to the flexibility they provide. But just like any good thing, if it is not well-regulated, it can easily deteriorate, which is why all the relevant stakeholders must put all hands-on deck to initiate and implement policies that guide the operations of hybrid and remote workers.

## Footnote

1. Cappelli, P., & Keller, J. R. (2019). Talent management: Conceptual approaches and practical challenges. Annual Review of Organizational Psychology and Organizational Behavior, 1, 305-331.

2. Dhanpat, N., Buthelezi, Z. P., Joe, M. M., Maphela, T. V., & Shongwe, N. (2019). Talent management and employee retention: Exploring options in a information technology organization in South Africa. SA Journal of Human Resource Management, 17, 1-9.

3. Schiemann, W. A. (2020). Reinventing talent management: Principles and practices for the new world of work. People and Strategy, 43(1), 15-21.

4. Collings, D. G., Mellahi, K., & Cascio, W. F. (2019). Global talent management and performance in multinational enterprises: A multilevel perspective. Journal of Management, 45(2), 540-566.

5. Gallardo-Gallardo, E., Dries, N., & González-Cruz, T. F. (2019). What is the meaning of 'talent' in the world of work? Human Resource Management Review, 23(4), 290-300.

6. Thunnissen, M., Gallardo-Gallardo, E., & Gómez-Cedeño, M. (2021). Towards a regional talent management framework: The case of Catalonia. International Journal of Human Resource Management, 32(15), 3063-3089.

7. Pham, N. T., Phan, Q. P. T., Tučková, Z., Vo, N., & Nguyen, L. H. L. (2020). Enhancing the organizational sustainable development of IT companies' employees: The roles of ethical leadership and cultural intelligence. Sustainability, 12(5), 1-18.

8. Pizam, A., Shapoval, V., & Ellis, T. (2021). Customer experience in hospitality: Global trends and new directions. International Journal of Hospitality Management, 88, 102574.

9. Adamsen, B. (2019). Talent management: A VUCA-driven world. Journal of Organizational Effectiveness: People and Performance, 6(2), 81-93.

10. Nijs, S., Gallardo-Gallardo, E., Dries, N., & Sels, L. (2021). A multidisciplinary review into the definition, operationalization, and measurement of talent. Journal of World Business, 49(2), 180-191.

11. Dhanpat, N., Madou, F. D., Lugisani, P., Mabojane, R., & Phiri, M. (2020). Exploring employee retention and intention to leave within a call centre. SA Journal of Human Resource Management, 16, 1-13.

12. Sabaitytė, J., Davidavičienė, V., & Straková, J. (2020). Digital transformation and new challenges in human resource management. E+M Ekonomie a Management, 23(2), 83-97.

13. Schlechter, A. F., Syce, C., & Bussin, M. (2021). Predicting intention to quit using demographic characteristics: An exploratory study in an aerospace organisation. SA Journal of Industrial Psychology, 40(1), 1-13.

# Chapter 10: Measuring Recruitment Effectiveness

*"Successful recruitment isn't just about filling roles quickly; it's about finding the right talent who contribute to our company's culture and growth."*

Looking at the realities of today's business environment, an effective recruitment process is among the huge determinants of a successful organization. Every organization, irrespective of size, location, and pedigree, needs to have the best people in order to thrive. Any organization that overlooks this concept pays dearly for it. I heard this story that happened two years ago about an IT consulting firm that was looking to hire a qualified full-stack engineer. So, they drafted a compelling job description and used all the available channels and platforms available at that point in time to advertise for the job role. Everything was going as planned; they got an influx of applications with exciting and promising resumes. So, they scheduled interview sessions for the prospective candidates. But unfortunately, as the interview sessions started, the HR and recruitment teams found out that none of the prospective candidates actually fit the bill. Yes, some of them possessed the needed skills and expertise, but their values, behaviours, and personalities didn't synch with the company's culture. So, assuming they go on to hire them, there will be a recurring personality clash in the organization, which in the long run will be detrimental to organizational growth and development. This, in my experience, is one of the regular challenges most organizations face, and it showcases the importance of measuring the effectiveness of the recruitment process.

Effective recruitment is not just any concept in talent acquisition and human resource management (HRM) in general; rather, it is one of the pillars of building a high-performing and competent workforce. With effective recruitment, you are not only certain that you have employed the best candidates; it also saves you time during the recruitment process and ultimately boosts your organization's overall productivity and success.

To further illustrate the power of effective recruitment, we will look at the story of Mrs. Sarah, who has been my mentor and leadership coach since I became a HR consultant. About five months ago, she was contracted to work as a HR manager at a fast-growing production company. According to her, she encountered a recruitment process that was not only haphazard but also lacked any meaningful recruitment metrics. This caused huge issues at the company because the HR team always struggled to get the best qualified candidates to fill any advertised vacancies. The task ahead was actually daunting, but she was very resolute to change the recruitment woes of the company. She started by analysing the company's recruitment strategy, having a thorough study of past recruitment, and analysing variables such as time-to-hire and employee retention rates. Her findings were mind-blowing; she discovered that the most successful hires had come from employee referrals, and those who had stayed with the company the longest were the ones who shared the company's core values.

Having all these valuable insights enabled her to make innovative changes to the company's recruitment process. She started by bringing on board her own HR and recruitment team, which helped her revamp and craft more compelling job descriptions that synced with the company's culture. In addition to that, she utilized employee brands and referrals to access a wider talent pool, while at the same time leveraging structured behavioural-based interview sessions to evaluate candidates' competencies. In order to evaluate the success of these changes, she started tracking key metrics and variables like the rate of candidate engagement, the rate of offer acceptance, and even first-year turnover. The results were commendable. Within the first year and six months, Mrs. Sarah and her recruitment team witnessed a surge in both the quantity and quality of prospective candidates, a drastic decline in time-to-hire, and a remarkable increase in the retention rate of new employees.

Mrs. Sarah's success story demonstrates how any organization can utilize the power of an effective recruitment process. All they have to do is understand the key recruitment metrics or employ someone who does, which will enable them to make data-driven decisions and optimize their hiring processes.

## Some of these key recruitment metrics include the following:

### Cost per hire

When we are talking about cost per hire as a key recruitment metric, it simply means the total cost of recruiting and hiring a new staff. One of the benefits of knowing the cost-per-hire (CPH) is that it helps an employer or organization fully grasp the financial cost of recruitment, which will help them to streamline and manage their recruitment budgets more efficiently.

If you wish to calculate CPH, it simply means summing up both the internal and external hiring and recruitment costs and dividing them by the number of hired employees. To get the figure, you have to take into consideration the cost of advertising on all the platforms and channels the job was posted on, the cost of contracting a HR and recruitment team, travel expenses during the interviews, the accommodation cost of housing the candidates throughout the duration of the interview, and also the time spent by the recruitment team during the hiring process. For example, if a company spent approximately $100,000 during the recruitment process over a period of six months and succeeded in hiring 10 new employees, their CPH would be $10,000. As a HR manager or recruiter, knowing the cost per hire is very important, especially if you have a budget to consider. This was the case of

Isaiah, who is the head of recruitment at Techyard, a struggling tech company in Nairobi. Techyard needed to hire cyber security experts to fill a vacant role within the company, and Isaiah was saddled with the responsibility of overseeing the recruitment process. He has to do this on a tight budget, so one of the key metrics he used was cost per hire. Isaiah carefully calculated all expenses involved in the recruitment process in order to ascertain how much it would cost on average to fill that position. By understanding this cost, Isaiah can identify areas where the company might be overspending and find ways to optimize the hiring process, ensuring that Techyard remains financially efficient while still attracting top talent.

## Source of Hire

Source for hire (SOH) is an important recruitment metric. It shows the origins of the prospective candidates and how these prospective candidates are sourced. The source in this context refers to channels such as social media platforms, recruitment and hiring agencies, past and current employee referrals, company websites, print media, and even campus recruiting. When an organization fully understands this metric, it helps the HR department strategically focus their attention and resources on the most effective channels and sources, thereby streamlining their hiring efficiency. During my time as the HR manager at Davis Consult, I noticed an interesting fact. There was this particular source that was attracting top talents who always did remarkable well in their job roles. So, I had to look into it by evaluating the source of the hire. What I discovered was that employee referrals, especially past employees, and LinkedIn were the best sources that were constantly bringing in top talents with competencies that aligned with the company culture and values. Also, these high-quality candidates that were sourced from these two sources had the lowest turnover rates in the company. So, all I had to do was focus my recruitment efforts and budget on the two sources.

## Time to hire

When we are talking about time to hire as a metric, what we are looking at is the exact time frame between when a job offer was posted and when the position was filled by a candidate. This metric is very important because it gives the HR or recruiter valuable insights into how effective and efficient their recruitment process is. To actually gauge this metric, the recruitment team has to effectively evaluate the organization's hiring process, starting from the point of screening resumes to the final part of scheduling interviews. This will help them identify any sort of bureaucratic bottleneck and other inefficiencies. Once these bottlenecks and inefficiencies have been identified, the next line of action will be to streamline the hiring process, improve communication with candidates, and leverage technology for quicker assessments, which will help to reduce the time to hire substantially. When an organization has a shorter time to hire, it means that such an organization can easily fill their vacant positions within the shortest possible time frame, thereby reducing the decline in productivity associated with the vacancies while at the same time securing the services of top talents before they are snatched by their competitors, giving them a competitive advantage over them.

## Candidate Experience

Candidate experience has to do with the candidate's perception of the entire hiring and recruitment process. From the application stage to the screening and interview sessions, and finally the boarding process. Prospective candidates are always observant of how they are treated during the whole hiring process, which also determines if they would be willing to work for the organization. Candidate experience is a way to gauge how effective your recruitment process is as an organization, and in addition to that, it also helps to improve your employer's brand and reputation, which is one of the indices that top talents look out for before agreeing to work for an organization. A negative candidate experience has a spiral effect on the organization's hiring process. It can deter potential candidates from working for the organization, and these candidates can also create bad PR for the company, putting the organization in a disadvantageous position when it comes to attracting and recruiting top talents. Companies that recognize the importance of candidate experience always prioritize establishing a good feedback mechanism for their prospective candidates, as it gives them the opportunity to get their opinions on the hiring process and how it can be improved upon.

## Offer Acceptance Rate

Whenever a firm puts out an advertisement for a job vacancy, their goal is to have those job vacancies filled by competent individuals. This ensures a continuous rhythm in the workflow, but unfortunately, some organizations find it difficult to get the best candidates to fill vacant positions in their departments even after placing so many job advertisements. So, this recruitment metric helps these organizations put things in a better perspective. When we are talking about the offer acceptance rate, we are simply calculating the percentage of job offers that were accepted by prospective candidates after the recruitment process had been carried out. How many candidates rejected the job, and for what reasons? How many candidates also accepted the job? To calculate the offer acceptance rate (OAR), you have to divide the number of accepted jobs by the total number of offers made before multiplying it by 100. One of the benefits of this recruitment metric is that it helps organizations redefine their recruitment process because it actually shows why candidates are declining the job offer. This can be due to many reasons, such as low and uncompetitive wages, an inflexible work schedule and lack of a conducive work environment, an unfavourable working environment, poor employer branding, and even a lack of well-defined organizational culture and values. Once the HR team is able to identify the reasons for the continuous decline in job acceptance, it becomes easy to fix the situation. One of the best ways to identify these reasons is to conduct an exit interview with candidates, especially the top talents who declined the job offer. The exit interview gives the HR team valuable insights on how to address the challenges in order to increase the organization's offer acceptance rate.

**Retention Rate.**

The retention rate has to do with the percentage of employees who continued to work for the organization over a specified period of time. In other words, it simply means the ability of an organization to retain and maintain a staple workforce. As we all know, the workforce is the engine room of any organization, and without them, no organization will make meaningful progress. The retention rate matrix is used by the HR department to critically evaluate the efficacy of the company's hiring and onboarding processes, as well as gauge overall employee satisfaction and engagement levels. Currently, most organizations are finding it a bit difficult to retain their top talents, mainly due to the competitive nature of the job market. Another pertinent issue that organizations are failing to consider is the age bracket of today's employees. The majority of today's employees are mostly Gen Z, while the remaining few are millennials. This group of employees are unique because of their perspective, reasoning, values, and goals. For example, I don't think there is a Gen Z employee who would want to continuously work in an organization that doesn't prioritize mental health, work-life balance, career development opportunities, a psychologically safe working environment, and competitive wage and benefits packages. So, if your organization is lacking in these aforementioned areas, your retention rate is likely to become very low because most of your employees will be on the lookout for better opportunities, and once they find any, they simply leave your organization. This not only disrupts the workflow and organizational growth but also has huge cost implications because all the investments and finances used in the recruitment and hiring process were lost shortly after onboarding.

**Endnotes**

1. Anderson, V. (2020). "Assessing the Impact of AI on Recruitment Processes." Journal of Human Resource Management, 35(4), 311-327.

2. Chapman, D. S., Uggerslev, K. L., Carroll, S. A., Piasentin, K. A., & Jones, D. A. (2021). "Applicant Attraction to Organizations and Job Choice: A Meta-Analytic Review of the Correlates of Recruiting Outcomes." Journal of Applied Psychology, 90(5), 928-944.

3. Bhatnagar, J., & Biswas, S. (2022). "Measuring Recruitment Effectiveness in the Digital Era: A Case Study Approach." International Journal of Human Resource Studies, 12(1), 45-62.

4. Marler, J. H., & Fisher, S. L. (2022). "The Effects of Technological Change on Recruitment and Selection." Journal of Business and Psychology, 37(2), 307-324.

5. Jones, K. P., King, E. B., Nelson, J., Geller, D. S., & Bowes-Sperry, L. (2020). "Beyond the Business Case: An Ethical Perspective of Diversity and Inclusion in Recruitment." Human Resource Management Review, 30(4), 100673.

6. Maurer, R., & Liu, Y. (2023). "Innovations in Recruitment Metrics: Moving Beyond Time-to-Hire and Cost-Per-Hire." HR Magazine, 68(2), 18-23.

7. Goldberg, C. B., & Allen, D. G. (2021). "Toward a More Comprehensive Understanding of Recruitment Effectiveness: The Role of Applicant Reactions." Academy of Management Annals, 15(2), 663-691.

8. Sullivan, J. (2021). "Data-Driven Recruitment: How Analytics are Transforming Hiring Practices." Journal of Workforce Analytics, 3(1), 15-29.

9. Bersin, J., & Chamorro-Premuzic, T. (2022). "The New HR Metrics: How AI is Reinventing Talent Acquisition." MIT Sloan Management Review, 63(3), 46-54.

10. Kaur, P., & Sharma, S. (2023). "Employee Referral Programs and Their Impact on Recruitment Effectiveness." Journal of Human Resources, 44(1), 102-120.

# Acknowledgement

I want to sincerely appreciate all the special people in my life who have contributed in some way to the success of this book. Their genuine encouragement, prayers, contributions, and advice helped me to put together this wonderful piece of knowledge. I'm grateful to the Almighty God for the wisdom, knowledge, and strength to pursue this dream and turn it into a reality.

I am especially grateful to my mentor and fellow HR consultant, Mrs. Sarah, for her guidance, corrections, patience, and insightful contribution, which were pivotal during the period of researching and writing this book.

I also want to thank my mother, Mrs. Chikwendu Maria, for her encouragement, prayers, and belief in me. She has always had faith in me and my work.

Finally, I dedicate this book to my late father.

www.ingramcontent.com/pod-product-compliance
Lightning Source LLC
Chambersburg PA
CBHW071950210526
45479CB00003B/884